ARCHERY COACHING How To's

ARCHERY COACHING
How To's

by Steve Ruis

Library of Congress
Cataloging-in Publication Data

Archery Coaching How To's / Steve Ruis.

p. cm
ISBN 978-0-9913326-0-1 (softcover)
1. Archery. 2. Coaching. 3. Training. I Steve Ruis 1946-

ISBN: 978-0-9913326-0-1

The web addresses cited in this text were current as of August 2013, unless otherwise noted.

Writer: Steve Ruis; **Copy Editor**: Steve Ruis; **Proofreader**: Michèle Hansen; **Cover Designer**: Steve Ruis; **Book Designer**: Steve Ruis; **Photographers** (cover and interior): Steve Ruis and Claudia Stevenson unless otherwise noted

Printed in the United States of America 10 9 8 7 6 5 4 3

Watching Arrows Fly
3712 North Broadway, #285
Chicago, IL 60613
312.505.9770
www.watchingarrowsfly.com

Contents

Introduction   1

How To's
Equipment

1. How to . . . Introduce Clickers   17
2. How to . . . Manage Draw Weight   25
3. How to . . . Teach Release Aids   37
4. How to . . . Introduce Slings   51
5. How to . . . Introduce Stabilizers   55
6. How to . . . Introduce Bow Sights   61
7. How to . . . Introduce Finger Tabs   69
8. How to . . . Introduce Peep Sights   75
9. How to . . . Introduce New Arrows   83

How To's
Form and Execution

10. How to . . . Teach the Use of Back Tension   93
11. How to . . . Teach Shooting Off of the Point   99
12. How to . . . Teach Stringwalking   107
13. How to . . . Introduce Different Anchors   115
14. How to . . . Teach a Finger Release   123
15. How to . . . Develop a Strong Bow Arm   129
16. How to . . . Create a Good Followthrough   133
17. How to . . . Create a Surprise Release
             (Compound)   139
18. How to . . . Adapt to New Bows   143
19. How to . . . Teach Relaxation   153

How To's
New Experiences

20. How to . . . Introduce Field Archery 161
21. How to . . . Introduce Target Archery 165
22. How to . . . Introduce Competition 169

Appendices

Having a Written Coaching Philosophy 179
Coaching Rationales 183
Mental Coaching Rationales 193
About the Author 204

Introduction

This book was born out of an idea that occurred to me while answering questions from a bunch of coaches I informally mentor. The problem was that for archers there are all kinds of "how to" books available in print and on the Internet, but for coaches there is hardly anything. Even the coach training courses focus on *what* to teach instead of *how* to teach it. So where should coaches go for ideas as to how to introduce various pieces of archery kit or new elements of form and execution? This volume is intended to fill some of that gap.

I am writing this for beginning-to-intermediate coaches and coaches who are coaching out of their specialty (*e.g.* compound coach with a recurve student).

My first encounter with this need was writing an article on how to introduce a clicker because I was less than impressed with the instructions that were available. Basically these instructions said: put the thingy on the bow and shoot until you get used to it. This was not at all satisfactory. How was I to know that a student was ready for a clicker? What was the best way to introduce the thing? How should my student train using it? None of these questions got answered in the references I could find, so I had to create my own procedure. The same is true for most of what else is in this book, which is an attempt on my part to provide you with guidance I did not have available.

It is important that you realize that what I have come up with is not "the way" to teach these things, but at least they are "a way" to teach them. If you have a better way, great, please take the time to publish it so that coaches will know that there is more than one way to coach that thing and if one is truly better than the others it should prove out over time. My hope is that future archery coaches will have all kinds of drills and suggestions as to how to teach the sport so that each of us doesn't have to "reinvent the wheel."

For each topic I will address:
- Is your athlete ready to learn this?
- How can you tell if they are ready?
- How do you introduce the topic?
- How do they drill/train with the new device/form element?
- What the pitfalls are and how to avoid them.

If you come up with a new protocol/teaching scheme for some element of archery, if you do nothing else please send it to me (*steve@archeryfocus.com*) and I will make sure it gets into print so other coaches can find it, try it, and recommend it to their peers (and, yes, give *you* credit).

General Caveats

Before we start with the teaching "how to's" please consider the following general caveats. Primary amongst them is that archery is an individual sport and the goal is for the archer to become independent. Independence does not mean "to be free from the need for coaching" but to be free to choose coaching or any other service the archer may feel is beneficial. Therefore we believe that you cannot lead archers to be independent by stripping away their independence. We, instead, believe the archer should make most of the decisions. On the other hand, some coaches are quite autocratic; it is "their way or the highway," so to speak. We do not believe this is in the best interests of the archer.

Some basic coaching approaches underlie all of our programs, including:

Basic Coaching Approaches

1. Safe archery practices must be taught, reinforced, and enforced in all stages of archery instruction. There are no exceptions.
2. All archers, no matter their age, need to begin archery with a very low draw-weight bow (10# draw for recurve, 15# draw for compound). Much of archery is learning how to achieve certain body positions, e.g. T-form at full draw while relaxed, yet under the tension of the draw. To encourage rapid progress, draw weight must be kept to a minimum at the beginning. The same is true when major changes to made to form—practice them initially at low draw weight and then work your way back up. If the student allows, instruction may begin with stretch bands or form straps.
3. Shooting should almost always begin up close at a fairly large target. The purpose is for archers of all levels to experience success, here in the form of the

arrows hitting the target. This is not a "lowering of the bar" but, at least in part, a training of the archer's self image to expect that their arrows will hit the target at or near the center. As an archer, young or old, progresses in developing consistent form, targets are moved farther away or switched out for smaller target faces at the same distance until the archer is shooting at standard-sized targets, at standard shooting distances.

4. Changes in *significant* parameters (draw weight, draw length, bow mass in the form of back weights, etc.) should be made in small increments, *e.g.* 2# of draw weight at a time, spread out over several shooting sessions. Large changes in such parameters distort good form, reversing progress.

5. Conversely, when adjusting less-significant parameters like body positions or accessory settings, make changes in large increments at first, followed by smaller ones. This is a manifestation of what I call *The Goldilocks' Principle* (This porridge is too hot! This porridge is too cold! This one is just right!). For example, if you are making a sight setting change because your arrows are hitting the target too high, you need to raise the aperture. Move it a half an inch or so. If that doesn't get you to center, move it another half of an inch. Often that first half an inch makes the arrows hit low instead—perfect! You now know the sight setting you are looking for is below the second one and above the first. Split that gap in half and retest. If the arrows are still "too low" split the difference again between the new mark and the "too

high mark"—you will be closer. In this manner, the changes get smaller and smaller until the setting is correct.

On the other hand, if you need to move the aperture up one whole inch and you only push it up $\frac{1}{16}$ of an inch, it will take you 16 tries to get it right.

The hard part for beginning coaches is to figure out what "a little" and "a lot" are—only experience will teach you that.

6. In all matters, it is recommended that coach and archer view each other as partners in achieving "better archery" for the archer. "Better archery" may mean having more fun, or getting better scores, or simply feeling better about participating. The archer sets the goal and the coach-student team works toward it via good communication. Coaches do not have to approve of the goal, but if you actually disapprove, you probably should not work with that archer.

7. We encourage all archers who are making equipment decisions to "Try Before You Buy." The history of archers buying unsuitable equipment and then developing bad form and execution in an attempt to force it to work for them is long and sad. It is important to know what is needed before going shopping. If you want to make good equipment recommendations, especially for youths, please educate yourself as to what is available and always be considerate of the archer's budget.

Basic Coaching Principles

- *Teach safety by building safe archery habits*, because

you don't have to think about a habit, it is just something you do.

- *If something creates pain, stop your athlete doing it!* This is only common sense . . . good common sense.
- *If your athlete practices something that is incorrect, it will take ten times the work doing it correctly to fix the improper execution.* This is not a scientific principle, just a fairly good rule of thumb. The point is we want to be able to trust our training and; in times of stress, it is easy to revert to other "options," therefore we don't want to practice those other options (also known as "bad habits").
- A key element in archery is achieving good form as quickly as possible because *archers do not want to practice doing it wrong!* Archers who receive solid coaching make very rapid progress due to this simple principle: If you don't pick up bad habits, you don't have to work to overcome them. Having said that, it is unwise to try to correct everything a beginning archer is not doing properly. The objective is to get students started well and then make corrections in their order of importance (generally in the order of their shot sequence) to get them into some semblance of good form rapidly.
- A basic rule of archery is: *never make more than one change at a time.* This is also the rule for adding new or different accessories. Why not? Because you won't be able to tell which change had which effect if you make more than one at a time.
- *The subconscious mind (responsible for the consistency of shot execution) cannot tell the difference*

6

between reality and something vividly imagined. This is the foundation for imagery and many other mental training techniques.

- While an archer is shooting, *if anything, anything at all—mental or physical—intrudes from a prior step, they must let down and start over.* This is the "Rule of Discipline" which is the foundation of a strong mental program. Archers willing to shoot shots they know aren't correct will not achieve any sort of consistent performance.

- A basic teaching principle is that *anytime you change something, your archery gets worse before it gets better.* Because archery is a repetition sport, archers have many repetitions of their usual shot making it feel comfortable and "normal." Any change feels uncomfortable and "abnormal" which automatically makes them worse. It takes a fair number of repetitions to overcome this effect and make the new way seem at least reasonable. If the "result" of the change is that an archer's shot gets worse and then gets better than when he started, it is a good change. If it gets worse and never gets back to where it was before, it is a bad change. So, we must give each change time to succeed before we pass judgement on it in order to make successful modifications to the shot.

- A key point is: *if they can group their arrows they can move that group into the center using aiming techniques.* If an archer can't group (a sign of inconsistent form), then aiming doesn't matter, so reasonable "grouping" must precede learning to aim.

Reasonable grouping comes from good form and relaxation.

- *If archers struggle to draw, they need less draw weight.* Too much draw weight can prevent good form from being created and can destroy good form already learned. Watch out for young males wanting to prove their manhood! Draw weight increases need to be gradual (two pounds or less (≤2#) at a time; see #4 above).

- *Stepwise procedures, such as for shooting arrows, need to be done emphasizing the separate steps in the beginning.* This is fundamental. There are physical and mental activities that accompany each step of the shooting process. If the steps are blended or slurred one into the next, the association of the physical and mental activities may be incorrect. Later, if archers experience trouble with their shot, reverting to the "fundamentals" is a diagnostic tool archers can use to fix problems.

- *You don't have to "do it right."* Some archers are obsessed with their shot being exactly as prescribed by this or that coach. This is neither healthy nor necessary. Just as every golfer's swing is uniquely his own, so is every archer's shot uniqueto its owner. There is a price to pay for using suboptimal form (less than the best possible form you are capable of) and that is extra training time. After that cost is paid, there may be no need to correct those "flaws." Consider the Olympic Recurve archer Michele Frangilli. He just won a gold medal at the 2012 London Olympics and has been representing Italy since 1996 at the Olympic Games. He also was the #1 ranked male Olympic Recurve archer for several years, yet his form is not what anyone would describe as being close to "textbook." There are, though, some form flaws that cost so many points they can't be practiced away, but these are few and far between. (But why create more work than necessary?)

Basic Aspects of Archery Practice

Here are a few simple principles that apply to all archery practice. You may want to share these with your students.

#1 *Don't practice shooting wrong.*

When you are just beginning, you are still learning how to shoot (or if you are rebuilding your shot, you are learning how to shoot differently). The jargon for this process is "finding your shot." Therefore, you don't want to shoot a great many arrows at this time since that is how you automate, or memorize, your shot. But you don't want to automate it until your shot is good, or you will end up memorizing wrong things. The rule is "get it right, *then* get it down."

You have to be focused on "learning your shot," which means you need to be trying to relax and feel all of the parts of your shot. There is a rule to help you in this: While you are shooting, *if anything, anything at all—mental or physical—intrudes from a prior step or from your environment, you must let down and start over.* I call this "the "Rule of Discipline." And, yes, I am repeating myself because if you

9

are willing to shoot shots that you know are not properly executed, you are giving your subconscious mind a license to improvise on the fly. Instead you want your subconscious mind to monitor your shots and blow a whistle when you do something differently from what you practiced. This rule applies in practice; this rule applies in competition. The closer you or your students adhere to this rule, the faster you will make progress.

#2 The form/execution element being worked on must be repeated more frequently than when just shooting normally.

Example If working on a new stance, don't just step up to the shooting line and empty your quiver. Step off the line after each shot and retake your stance. *Example* If your draw needs work, try "Double Draws." This involves drawing to take a shot, then letting down almost to brace (or to brace if a compound with letoff is being shot), then drawing a second time and then finishing the shot.

#3 The only basis upon which a practice exercise/shot should be evaluated is the element being worked on.

Example If you are working on having a soft, repeatable bow hand and you lose focus and put an arrow through an air conditioning duct, but your bow hand was nice and soft, that was a "good shot." This is why expert archers shoot without a target face (blank bale or even blind bale, i.e. with eyes closed) when working on form/execution elements. The target automatically supplies a judgment system that has nothing to do with what is being worked on. Do not give yourself mixed messages when you are working on your form and execution! Follow this rule, instead, and you will make rapid progress.

#4 *Often when you make a significant change things get worse before they get better.*
Generally this is a matter of focus. The new form/execution element attracts so much of your attention that you lose some on other aspects of your shot. The only true measure of whether a change is successful is whether your quality indicators (practice scores, group sizes, etc.) get better after getting worse when you make the change. There is an oft-quoted adage that "it takes 21 days of practice to create a new habit." There is no scientific evidence for this, but it serves as a reasonable (probably minimal) guideline. (The Navy Seals say "eight weeks.")

#5 *The most important aspect of archery to practice is relaxation.*
To be successful, archers need to be able to relax and focus under the tension of the draw. Muscles that are tensed but don't need to be sap your energy, reduce your flexibility, and contribute to tension elsewhere in your body, including in your mind.

#6 *If you want your mental program to work in competition, it must be a regular part of your practice.*
This may sound obvious but the vast majority of archers don't do it. This is a major topic in itself and beyond the

11

scope of this volume, so more on mental practice will have to be found elsewhere. (For a gentle beginning consider "Why You Suck at Archery" by yours truly and for a more indepth look try my 'Winning Archery" or "With Winning in Mind" by Lanny Bassham.)

Here are some additional key points regarding practice:

- The term "practice" stands for so many things to different people that there is great confusion among archers about what it means, so beware of advice from others.
- If you don't know specifically why you are practicing, you are probably wasting your time and quite probably deluding yourself.
- Never, ever practice doing something you know is wrong; fix it first. (This is an aspect of what is called "deliberate practice.")
- Practicing for a set number of shots or for a set time cannot be right, let alone is right. Practice to a purpose, not a number.
- A successful practice is one in which you accomplished what you were trying to accomplish. ("Achieve, then leave." Jack Nicklaus)
- It is very easy to deceive yourself, which is why you need an outside point of view (from a coach or experienced shooting partner).
- Bring your goals to you by using larger targets at shorter distances and practice being successful by shooting high score after high score, working your way back to standard distances and standard size targets.

Author's Note

For you amateur or professional grammarians out there who think the title should have used "how-tos" or "how tos," or "how toes" or any of the other variants, I researched this usage and decided to use the variant used by *The New York Times*. But if you feel strongly about the choice, please do write me about it at *steve@archery-focus.com*.

SPR

Steve Ruis

How To's . . .

Equipment

A clicker is a spring or magnetically sprung rod or blade that slides atop the arrow as it is drawn. When the arrow reaches full draw the clicker rod/blade slides off and makes a "click" telling the archer that they are at the same draw as the previous shot. Clickers must be carefully set to coincide with the full-draw-position of the archer.

1
How To . . .
Introduce a Clicker

General Background Information

By all accounts a gentlemen by the name of Fred Leder invented the clicker. His idea was to get away from using his eye as a triggering mechanism and instead to use his ears with an audio trigger. In late 1957, he experimented and practiced in his basement archery range and, by the next spring, he was competing with the best in the area. In 1961 at the NFAA National Field Championships in Crystal Springs, Arkansas Earl Hoyt took notice and Hoyt Archery started selling clickers. (*Primary*   *Source* http://home.fuse.net/k8cxm/clicker.htm)

As far as their use goes, there was a great deal of experimentation. Originally some archers used it as just a draw check and held for several seconds after the "click" occurred, rather than use it as a sign to release the string. Modern technique requires that an archer be in complete control of their clicker, meaning that when the clicker "clicks" the shot is loosed only if all of the other criteria for a good shot are met. The sound of the clicker alone cannot be used as a signal as then stray clicking noises can confound your archer; it is a combination of sound *and* feel that is the signal.

You must not teach to a conditioned reflex, which is when an archer looses whenever the clicker "clicks" no matter what. The training procedure below includes a process that requires some time between the "click" and the loose (which allows for the unconscious check mentioned), which shortens with training so that the loose follows the "click" *almost* immediately.

Clickers are generally used by Olympic Recurve archers but are also used by Compound-Fingers archers, and even a few traditional archers. Some coaches put clickers on the bows of archers struggling with target panic. This is not recommended as a "cure," but it can help.

How Do I Know My Athlete Is Ready for a Clicker?
Beginners should shoot barebow until they have fairly consistent form. Then, if they want to shoot a clicker or if you think they are ready, do the following test.

A Clicker Readiness Test
The student draws on target and settles in. When their arrow stops moving (back, only back; if it saws back and forth, they aren't ready) put a dot on the arrow shaft opposite their rest hole/plunger with a suitable marking pen (black or silver

Sharpie, whatever). Then they let down. Ask them to relax, take a breath and repeat. This is done 5-6 times resulting in 5-6 dots on the arrow shaft. Then show the student the shaft. What is desired is to see the farthest dots no more than a half inch apart. If they are more than one inch apart, the student is not ready for a clicker. At a half inch or shorter, the archer is definitely ready. Between the half inch spread and one inch spread, it is your call. If the student is in a rush to be a champion, make him wait. If the student is diligent, patient, and hard working go ahead with the clicker.

This is obviously a test for draw length consistency. Do not introduce a clicker until an archer has a fair degree of form consistency because if that is lacking, trying to learn a clicker will be very frustrating. If you know any clicker stories, they all center on the frustration of using the danged thing.

Fine Point You can use any part of the bow as a reference to make the dots as long as you are consistent.

How to Get Started (Clicker)

Basic Setup First you need be select a good starting point for the position of the clicker. An excellent place is at the tip of the arrow when the spread of dots on that shaft is centered on the plunger or slightly ahead of their center when the arrow is drawn (or just held in that position). Adjustments will need to be made, of course, but this is a good starting point.

What you want to avoid is giving a clicker to a student with a one inch or longer spread in arrow point location. This will be discouraging because about one sixth of the time, the clicker will work as you want it to, but one-half of the time the student will pull right through the clicker on the way to anchor, necessitating a "do over," and another one third of the time, the student will be so short at anchor that they can't get through the clicker at all and have to let down.

You want your students to practice *succeeding using the clicker*, and five failures out of six tries is neither good practice nor success. The resulting frustration can put off an otherwise eager archer.

Training (Clicker)

Initial Stages Start by stripping sight and stabilizer(s) off of the athlete's bow (to avoid distractions), then have them step up to an empty target butt (also called a "blank bale"). The coach directs how this will go. The athlete slides an arrow under the clicker and then you ask him to draw the arrow while watching the clicker. Your goal is to get them to a correct full-draw-position with the clicker still on the arrow but quite near its falling off point. Adjustments may have to be made.

A Potential Pitfall A pitfall to avoid when learning to draw with a clicker on the bow is using the clicker to determine where full draw is. This is a mistake. Full draw needs to be determined by feel and confirmed by the clicker. To avoid this, you may need the archer to draw with his eyes closed from time to time.

Next you instruct the archer to draw to full draw (watching the clicker) and then "finish the shot" by extending to the target with their bow arm and rotating their rear shoulder toward their back. But finishing the shot will consist of various instructions during training; here they are:

Training Script
After the Clicker "Clicks," You Will . . .

Let Down
Release
Let Down
Wait 1 sec and Release
Let Down
Release
Let Down
Wait 2 sec and Let Down
Let Down
Wait 3 sec and Let Down
Let Down

.

.

.

(as the list grows the number of let downs shrinks from every other one to every fourth or fifth one)

A parent or friend can read the instructions as they are practicing or they can just tape up the list within sight while practicing. This training can be tedious, so it is okay to take a break and shoot without the clicker for a while.

Also, if your athlete is still growing, the position of the clicker will need to be adjusted often. It also needs to be adjusted if the equipment is changed and if your athlete's form isn't fairly solid which is why you should wait until some draw length consistency exists before introducing the clicker.

Later Stages After some control over the use of the clicker is achieved, indicated by the student-archer becoming relaxed when using it, rarely pulling through, etc. then transition to normal use without the training script.

Potential Pitfalls (Clicker)

1. *Using the Clicker to Determine Full Draw* (see above)
2. *Clicker Problems Causing Tension*

It is not uncommon for new clicker users to encounter some difficulty in a tournament. Tournaments foster tension and tension shortens muscles, which makes it harder to get through the clicker. Difficulty getting through the clicker creates yet more tension making it even harder to get through the clicker and a positive feedback loop is created. (Ack!) Archers need to know that when they encounter difficulty getting through their clicker, what they need to do is *relax*. Focusing on the feeling of their draw arm and hand stretching during the draw can help (the feeling is an illusion but it is real). Young athletes are especially blind-sided by this as their focus is elsewhere (scoring, winning, etc.). If this happens to one of your archers, tell them it is okay to shoot without the clicker, either for a while (until they relax) or for the rest of the tournament. Don't make a big deal of it. Certainly don't ask them to force their way through the problem.

3. *Beware of Clicker Cheats*

There are myriad "clicker cheats," i.e. ways for your archer to get the arrow point through the clicker without proper form and execution. One such "cheat" is extending the bow wrist (moving from a relaxed bow wrist to a "high" wrist will move the bow slightly farther away). Another is curling the fingers of the draw hand, as when "making a fist." A list all of these is too long to include here. Be aware that clicker cheats are often introduced subconsciously as a temporary fix for "not coming through the clicker easily" and if adopted under tournament pressure, that pressure can burn that form flaw into an archer's form in short order. Much work will need to be done to overcome such high intensity practice (malpractice?).

2
How To . . .
Manage Draw Weight

General Background Information

There is shockingly little in the general archery literature about managing draw weight. Here are the reasons for and against more and less draw weight.

More Draw Weight At any given draw length, a higher draw weight gives an archer's arrows flatter trajectories and less time of flight due to higher arrow speeds. The less time of flight means wind has less time to act on the arrow which is good. The higher arrow speed means distance marks on a sight are closer together (making misreading or missetting the sight a smaller mistake). The flatter trajectory means that the archer is closer to level T-form even on longer shots, because the higher the bow needs to be held, the harder it is to maintain good form.

On the negative side, more draw weight requires the archer to expend more energy in drawing the string and holding it at full draw. As a rule of thumb archers working on their form need minimum draw weights and "poundage" should only be added in small increments (≤2#) while maintaining good form and execution.

Less Draw Weight At any given draw length, a lower draw weight gives an archer's arrows a higher trajectory and more time of flight due to lower arrow speeds. The greater time of flight means wind has more time to act on the arrow which is not good. The lower arrow speed means distance marks on a sight are farther apart (making misreading or missetting the sight a larger mistake) and possibly even having marks so extremely far apart that the sight interferes with the arrow or the archer loses sight of the aperture through the sight window (this is often the case for archers who are young and adults with very short draw lengths). The higher trajectory means that the archer is farther from level T-form on longer shots, and again, the higher the bow is held, the harder it is to maintain good form.

Less draw weight, however, is desirable when an archer is over-bowed (forcing them to distort good form and use muscles not conducive to good shooting) or when they decide to make major changes in their shot. Learning needs to be done at the lowest draw weight possible.

Draw weights that are too low can make it very difficult to reach longer targets with consistent execution, even using all of the tricks of the trade.

How Do I Know My Athlete Is Ready
for a Draw Weight Change?

This will be broken down into Recurve and Compound recommendations because the weight changes are different, as are the tests for readiness.

We urge you to establish that there is a valid need for higher draw weight before recommending one. An example of a good reason is trying to meet the minimum draw weight to go bowhunting. An unfortunate and endemic problem with younger male archers is trying to draw more weight for bragging rights amongst their peers. This is not a good reason. Realize that draw weight changes of just a few pounds can require the purchase and tuning of new arrows as well as the purchase of new limbs or, in the case of compound bows, even a new bow, so this can be expensive as well as time consuming.

Here are some tests that can be used to determine readiness for a draw weight increase.

A Higher Draw Weight Readiness Test
(Recurve Bows)

Have your student draw her bow to anchor, hold for seven seconds comfortably, then let down to predraw position for two seconds, then repeat. If she can do this eight times in succession without strain, her draw weight is correct. If she can only do this 3-4 times, it will be difficult to learn to shoot well. If she can do this ten or more times, her draw weight can be increased.

This test was developed by Coach Kim, H.T. of Korea

Draw Weight Appropriateness Test (Compound Bows)

Your student must be able to draw the bow comfortably with the arrow leveled at a target with no grimacing or other outward sign of excessive effort. If you think your student is faking it, they should also be able to do this while sitting in a chair.

Archers should be able to shoot comfortably like this for many dozens of arrows. If so, your archer can advance to a higher draw weight.

Fine Point The recurve bow test can be used for longbows, too.

How to Get Started (Draw Weight Change)

Recurve Bows Your student (or student's parents if underage) needs to be told that new limbs may need to be purchased (even a new bow if student is shooting a one-piece recurve or longbow) and that new arrows may be needed as well. At the very minimum, new sight marks (or gaps, points of aim (POAs), or crawls for barebow archers) will be necessary with the new limbs or bow.

Three-piece recurve bows with adjustable limb pockets have adjustable draw weights. The most common system is the ILF (for International Limb Fitting; *see the sidebar* "Where Did the ILF System Come From?"). This system allows for the reduction of the maximum draw weight (listed on the limb) of an ILF bow by roughly 10%. So, if the bow is 20# @ 28", by backing out the limbs all of the way (roughly four full turns but may be more), you will have an 18# @ 28" bow. Each of the "turns" on the limb bolts in this case equates to one-half pound of draw force (*see the sidebar* "What Does Turning the Limb Bolts Really Do?"). For a 40# bow, those figures would be: 36# with the bolts all of the way out, each turn equating to one whole pound of draw force.

To increase draw weight add a whole turn (downward) to both the upper and lower limb bolts (on better bows this can be done while strung, but don't count on it with all bows) and have your student shoot some arrows. If they are completely comfortable at this new draw weight, add additional turns or fractions of turns (the same to each bolt to preserve any tiller setting), but no more than equate to a 2# increase in draw weight at one time.

Realize that not all limbs and limb pockets are the same shape, nor are they the same quality, so you may find that some limbs don't fit into the limb fittings when the limb bolts are quite far out. However, all should fit when the limbs are all of the way in.

What If There Are No More Turns Available? This means the current limbs are "maxed out," so the only way to add draw weight is to get new limbs. Some coaches have several pairs of limbs to loan out to students temporarily while they are figuring out what their new draw weight will be, but there is also a lively secondary market in used limbs because everybody grows out of several pairs of limbs while gaining strength and form. Have your student ask around.

With the recommended two pound limit on draw weight changes and limbs being sold in 2# increments (14#, 16#, 18#, 20#, etc.) you might expect that the next set of limbs should be 2# heavier. Instead, because of the adjustability built into the ILF system, your student needs limbs that are 4# heavier. In the example of the 20# bow backed off to 18#, and when the limbs are bottomed out (to 20#), if your student acquires 24# limbs (4# heavier), when installed and backed out all of the way, they will be 21.5# (24# – 10% = 21.5#) which is less than a two pound increase over their old draw weight of 20#. Later these limbs can be cranked down to the nominal 24# of draw. With ILF limb fittings limbs have to be changed only half as often as without them. This is a major cost savings.

Compound Bows While recurve bows, at least those with adjustable limb pockets, have 10% of maximum draw weight adjustments available, compound bows typically have 25% of peak weight adjustability (and newer ultra-adjustable compound bows have draw weight ranges as large as 5-70#—but not all draw weights are available at each draw length). This means that adjusting the draw weight is usually a matter of turning the limb bolts in or out a turn or so at a time.

What If There Are No More Turns Available? This means either a new bow or an expensive limb upgrade (often requiring new limbs, new eccentrics, and new string and cables, plus quite a bit of labor) is required. Consider that compound bows have quite long service lives and can be handed down or sold on the secondary market, offsetting the cost of a new bow.

Fine Points When purchasing a compound bow, archers who are still developing their form must acquire a bow with a draw weight range whose *minimum* is close to what they are pulling now. This gives a lot of room to move up in draw weight. Moving up is normal. If a bow has a maximum specification at what they are pulling now, the only way to move up is either a new bow or the expensive limb upgrade (described above).

Training (Draw Weight Change)

Initial Stages Archers must get used to a new draw weight and it might take several weeks of shooting at the new value for it to feel "normal." During this time, all previous sight marks are changed but it is probably not wise to sight in again as another draw weight change may be coming. As a general rule, all draw weight changes need to be made and shot in before these other issues are adjusted; typically this shooting is done blank bale.

This is one of the few cases in which shooting a particular number of arrows per shooting session is helpful. Until quite a few shots are logged, the new draw weight will not feel normal.

Later Stages After your archer is comfortable with the final new draw weight setting, a great many things need to be checked or adjusted:

- *arrow suitability* (bare shaft test or other)
  New arrows may need to be purchased or old arrows may need to be shortened (which then affects things like clicker position and/or arrow rest position).
- *bow string suitability* (recurve)
  The number of strands in a recurve bow string are

determined by draw weight, so a string with more strands may be necessary. More strands means thicker strings which therefore affect nock fit, so that must be addressed, too.

- *sight marks*
  Whatever sighting system is being used, a new set of marks needs to be acquired.

Potential Pitfalls (Draw Weight Change)

1. *Overstressed Archers*

Coaches must be on the lookout as to whether their archer-athlete's new draw weight is overstressing them. If their form starts to break down or they show signs of struggling to draw their bow, back off the last draw weight change. Make changes in smaller increments or put them off for awhile. Some athletes can feel rushed by such changes and can act out their unhappiness while saying little if anything.

2. *Overstressed Family Budgets*

Families with young archers, especially those with more than one young archer, can find their "recreation budgets" overstressed this process. A recurve archer needing new limbs and new arrows can spend hundreds of dollars in very little time. Be sure to talk to your athletes and their families (if someone else is paying the bills) about what the potential costs can be. Coaches who are sensitive to these stresses on the family budget will find appreciative archers and grateful parents.

What Does Turning the Limb Bolts Really Do?

When limb bolts are turned, the angle that the limb makes with the bow changes. This seemingly small adjustment affects quite a few things, the two most important are:

1. *The distance the string is from the bow (brace height)*
When the string is farther from the bow (bolts moved out), it travels less distance to reach full draw position (this measurement is called the power stroke) which means the arrow spends less time on the string when loosed, which in turn lowers its speed. The reverse happens when the bolts are moved in.

2. *The angle the string makes with the limb*
The more vertical the limb, the more the limb flexes as the string is pulled back to full draw position, which increases the peak draw weight, arrow speed, etc. Screwing in the limb bolt makes the limb more vertical, screwing it out makes it less vertical.

If the limb bolts are not locked in place somehow, it is wise to place a mark on the top of the bolt, aligned with the limb, so that if vibration causes them to move, this can be observed and the bolts reset. Many recurve and compound bows have set screws that are used to lock limb bolts down so they do not do this. Consequently these set screws need to be loosened to make changes in limb bolt position and then retightened.

Also, if one limb bolt is change differently from the other, the nocking point locator(s) is moved. You will need to reset it.

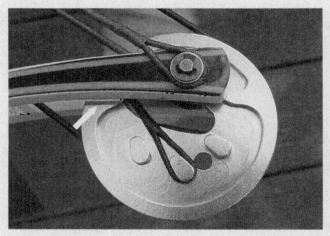

Compound archers mark their limb bolts! Make a mark on each bolt head that lines up with the limb. In that way if the bolt vibrates around you can note it. Also, marks are made on the bow's eccentrics/wheels (usually lined up with the edge of the limb—see arrow in photo) to provide the same indicator. If a limb bolt moves, the mark moves.

Where Did the ILF System Come From?

The International Limb Fitting (ILF) system (*see photo*) was a brilliant invention which then got adopted worldwide. Unfortunately this was not done by the inventor, but through piracy. The ILF system was invented by Hoyt Archery and was *then copied without permission or compensation, by other manufacturers around the world.* Rather than be embroiled in lawsuits forever, Hoyt did not vigorously contest this patent infringement and *voilà,* a new world standard was born. Virtually every manufacturer of recurve bow limbs makes some, if not all, of its limbs to this specification. Archers have benefited tremendously from this, so the next time you see somebody from Hoyt Archery, thank them.

The ILF limb system! Not only do the limbs just clip in (instead of being screwed on with the limb bolts) but they are adjustable for draw weight and often limb position, too.

Release aids can be strapped to your wrist and triggered with your index finger (center), held in your hand and triggered with your thumb (top left and bottom right) or held in your hand and set off without a trigger (bottom left and top right).

3
How to . . .
Teach Release Aids

General Background Information

Release aids are mechanical triggers that replace an archer's fingers on a bow string. Their use dates back thousands of years but the first modern release aids date back the 1960's or so (even though one was patented in the U.S. in 1879, widespread use took almost another century). The early releases were straps or handheld devices with a lip to catch on the bowstring which then fell off when the device was rotated. In the 1970's release aids with internal mechanisms became prevalent. Today there are hundreds of different designs. For now we will split them into two broad classes: *handheld release aids* (preferred by target archers) and *wriststrap release aids* (preferred by bowhunters) although any release aid can be used for almost any purpose (*see photos*).

Release aids in competitive target archery are officially confined to their use with compound bows, even though you could use one with a recurve bow, if you were willing to compete against compound archers. Therefore this is basically a compound bow topic. (Whatever you want to do for fun (release with longbow, etc.) is up to you.)

How Do I Know My Athlete Is Ready for a Release Aid?

This isn't so much of a piece of equipment one needs to be ready for, but a matter of personal preference. The highest scores being shot are with compound bows and release aids and some are attracted to that.

Having said that, beginning archers learn best when what they need to know is learned in stages. Some archer-parents, though, equip their children with full compound kit (bow, release aid, telescopic sight, peep sight, stabilizers, etc.) right from the start and are successful in teaching their children how to shoot. It is very difficult, however, to help a new archer with full freestyle equipment without a lot of very personal attention. All of that equipment has to be fitted. If the archer is young, the weight of a compound bow alone may be a bit too heavy to shoot well, and when a bunch of accessories get bolted on, the rig becomes prohibitively heavy. This is a questionable approach at best. And while parents are there every time their child shoots, coaches generally are not. Trying to learn a great many things simultaneously can be done but is quite difficult to do, especially when a coach doesn't see an athlete for a week or more between sessions.

It is better to have a young archer shooting with a bare bow, then with stabilizer(s) added, sight added, and peep, etc. with their fingers on the string before a release aid is introduced. Basic form is learned barebow, then a stabilizer is added, then bow sight, then a peep sight and adjustments are made to adapt to each. (Tab, sling, quiver, etc. are introduced along the way.)

How to Get Started (Release Aid)

Basic Setup The hard part is getting a suitable release to practice with. There are many styles, sizes, mechanisms, etc. and they are not inexpensive. Beginners are best started with a triggerless handheld release aid as these are less expensive and better to train on. Whatever the release aid, the key points are that (a) the release must be of a size to fit the archer's hand and (b) set up so that it triggers at an appropriate place. If you are not adept at doing this, get professional help, either from an archery shop technician or a proficient compound archer.

It Has to Fit Both Ways Not only does a release aid need to fit an archer physically (if a wrist-strap is involved, the release head has to be adjustable on its shaft so the trigger falls under your student's finger (not fingertip) when relaxed; handhelds need to fall between your student's fingers when their hand is relaxed, etc.); it also has to fit them *mentally*. If your archer is laid back and doesn't get too excited, they should be fine with a trigger release. If they are kind of nervous and flighty, then maybe they would be better off with a triggerless release.

How do you know which they are? This is difficult, so they may have to try several styles before they find one that really works well for them. Release shooters often ask their peers to try out their releases. This testing should always be done with a rope bow (described below; for safety) and is one good way to find out whether a particular model is worth further investigation. In the final analysis, whether or not your archer will like a release aid is a personal decision.

Preparing for Training (Release Aid)

Safety Note Archers who learned to shoot with a release aid and who started training using their bows all have stories of the release going off prematurely and having their release hand come flying back to smack them in the face. Archers have been knocked out this way and have lost teeth doing this. Archers should never begin release training with a bow in hand, either with their first release aid or with any subsequent new release aid. The negative effects of a premature release can retard progress a great deal.

Archers must begin with a "rope bow," which is made from a piece of nonstretching parachute cord or ⅛″–³⁄₁₆″ nylon rope knotted together at the ends to make a loop. This has to be tied such that when the loop is placed over the bow hand, and attached to the release aid it extends out

to the archer's exact draw length when in their full-draw-position.   Exact means exact; too long or too short will not do. The archer's full draw form  should be exactly the same as when they have their bow in hand.

Next, the archer assumes full draw position, and the coach addresses the archer's release hand position and touch point. To find your archer's beginning draw hand position, have them rotate their release wrist as far as it will go in both directions while in full draw position (*see photos right*). Then have them find a position about half way in between the two extreme positions of rotation. Typically this is 10-15° from level. This should be close to the most comfortable position for the archer's arm, hand, and wrist. Then the archer needs to become familiar with his "touch point." The release hand should touch the face somewhere. (When first developed release aids were often taught with a "floating anchor." It seems strange now (*see photo right*) but bows weren't all that fast then, and having a much lower anchor position, even if floating, gave considerable distance to shots.) The archer's touch point varies slightly with

To find the correct hand angle find the point half-way between the extremes of rotation. This can be done with or without a rope bow.

distance shot when a peep sight is introduced, so students

should not be taught that they must have a "consistent anchor position" as when they shoot without a peep sight.

Training (Release Aid)

Phase 1 When the student is ready and at full-draw-position, he places a small amount of tension on the loop and then, under the guidance of the coach,

By all means avoid the dreaded "floating anchor" (in which the release hand has no "touch point").

actuates the release. This needs to coincide with the student's draw elbow lining up exactly with the vertical plane of the arrow while it is swinging around toward his back in an arc. If this is done properly, the rope loop should shoot out a couple of feet and land on the floor. If it just droops from the bow hand or falls to the floor just below the bow hand, it was a poor release. Your student needs enough tension to simulate the draw weight in hand (the holding weight) of the compound bow and to obtain a "clean release."

Students need to work with the string loop until they can work the release aid, on demand and without fail, using the rope bow. Generally this takes several shooting sessions. The archer is allowed to shoot his/her bow in addition, but not with the release aid. The rope bow is for training, but it will get boring if that is all they do.

Phase 2 Once the rope loop has been mastered, the bow becomes involved. Note that the student's draw length probably will need to be adjusted, but first a D-loop should be affixed to the bow string (*see the sidebar* "How to Tie a D-Loop"). Some archers would rather use a rope on the release while others prefer to attach the release directly to the bowstring; that is their choice. A D-loop prevents wear and tear on the bowstring and has many other advantages, so it should be highly recommended. Now, the draw length is adjusted to give the archer the correct draw length, a comfortable draw hand position, and a recognizable touch point for that hand.

A Potential Pitfall Because compound bows reach full draw weight near the three-quarters point of the draw stroke, accidentally triggering the release at that point will result in a surprise—a nasty surprise. The archer's draw hand will come flying back, often colliding with the archer's face. (Archers with dental braces obviously need to be especially cautious.) For this reason, if your archer is using a trigger release, the triggering appendage needs to be tucked away while drawing. For wrist-strap releases, the index finger is tucked behind the trigger, only to be swung on top when at anchor. For thumb triggers, the thumb is usually held out away from the trigger until full-draw-position and anchor are achieved.

Students should then stand close to a blank bale and experience shooting arrows with their eyes closed. This can be disconcerting for the first few arrows because the feel and sound of the bow being discharged is quite dramatically different from shooting a rope bow. After a dozen or so shots, have the student shoot a few more with eyes open.

If the archer experiences any difficulties at all (flinches, poor timing, punching the trigger, etc.) send them back to the rope bow to reacquire the correct feel and technique. In these circumstances, make sure that the draw length and release speed are properly adjusted. Don't blame your archer for an equipment flaw.

Next, comes sighting in with their new setup. None of their previous sight marks are any good now, so start up close.

Potential Pitfalls (Release Aid)

1. *Premature Releases*

Because compound bows reach full draw weight near the three-quarters point of the draw stroke, triggering the release at that point will result in a surprise, an unpleasant surprise. The archer's draw hand will come flying back, often colliding with the archer's face. (Archers with dental braces need to be especially cautious for obvious reasons.) For this reason, if your archer is using a trigger release, the triggering appendage needs to be tucked away while drawing. For wriststrap releases, the index finger is tucker behind the trigger, only to be swung on top when at anchor. For thumb triggers, the thumb is usually held out away from the trigger until full draw position and anchor are achieved.

2. *Punching, et al.*

There are myriad flaws in using release aids, primary amongst these is willfully triggering the release, called "punching" the release. Match rifles have stiff triggers on them that are squeezed until the rifle goes off. There is no movement of the trigger (called trigger "throw") that lets the shooter know the rifle is going to fire. If there is, the shooter's mind anticipates the trigger position that sets the gun off and tends to flinch in an attempt to brace for the explosion. The same is true for release using archers. The trigger must just be squeezed while aiming is concentrated on and the release goes off when it goes off. Eventually a rhythm is established and the release goes off within a narrow band of time after anchor.

3. *Hair Triggers*

Some archers seem to think that setting their triggers to their most sensitive settings (creating a "hair trigger") is a good idea. It is not. Archers who cannot rest their finger/thumb on their trigger without fear the thing is going to go off will not shoot well. Similarly archers who are afraid their triggerless release aids are going to go off while they are drawing will not shoot well. Set the triggers to their heavier settings and triggerless release aids so that they will only fire when the archer's wrist and draw arm are properly positioned behind the arrow.

How to Tie a D-Loop

(*I learned this method of tying D-loops from George Chapman who recently passed away and is greatly missed.*) First, why a D-loop? Before D-loops, archers had "release ropes," a section of cord tied to the release itself that wrapped arround the bowstring and then went back to the release. From the photo below you can see that this placed a great deal of downward pressure on one's arrow rest, not a good thing. There are lots of other reasons to use a D-loop, which is why almost everyone does now.

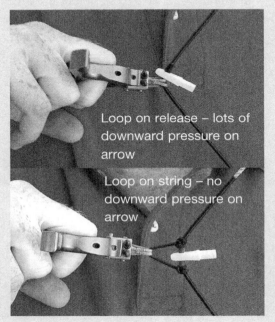

Loop on release – lots of downward pressure on arrow

Loop on string – no downward pressure on arrow

Tying a D-loop

There are many ways to do this, this particular way is nice because you can prepare a bit of cord ahead of time and carry it without out onto a field course and, if needed, replace your loop with little fuss.

Step 1 Cut the loop material (release rope) to length and melt the ends (making small balls) first. Typical loops are 4½ or 4¾ inches long. The ends can be melted with a match or lighter (*see photo*).

Step 2 Make a loop behind the bowstring and feed both ends through. Then pull the one closest to the nocking point up, feeding the other one in as you pull. There's the first knot (*see photos below left*).

Step 3 Then the long string is placed on the other

side of the bowstring, wrapped around the string, up and around itself and then tucked in to make the second loop (*see photos next page*). You can use the other knot as a pattern to make a mirror image of the first knot.

Step 4 To set the loop, insert the noses of needle nosed pliers into the loop and pull *open* the jaws (slowly, making sure the knots get cinched up evenly and they don't come loose).

Where to Place the D Loop

Some still use tied on nocking

points (upper and lower) and tie the loop outside of those (*see first photo*). Some people use the D-loop as upper and lower nocking points. Some use just an upper nocking point with the loop and some are using just a bottom nocking point with their loops. It won't hurt to try these different configurations, but do realize that many of these configurations change the position of the arrow at anchor in that you may be anchoring in the same place, but you are pulling from a different position behind the arrow. If you lower the nock relative to your anchor, you will get

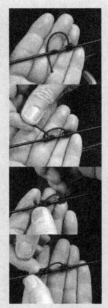

more distance. If you raise it, you will get the opposite. site.

What is a Back Tension Release Aid?

You will read of "back tension release aids." This is a misnomer. When triggerless mechanical releases were first developed it was felt that they *required* the use of back tension to set them off, hence the name. They were wrong. No release can require back tension for its use. *All release aids can be shot with or without back tension.* When you see the term "back tension release" it generally means "triggerless release."

The first mechanical triggerless release aid, the Stanislawski release, loving called "the Stan" by those who won with it. This is a three finger model; many preferred the two finger model.

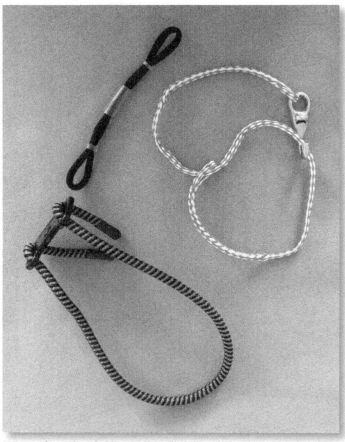

Finger Slings (top left) attach to thumb and forefinger. Wrist Slings (top right) attach to the bow wrist and connect back to themselves. Bow Slings (bottom left) attach to the bow.

4

How To . . .
Introduce Slings

General Background Information

Contrary to popular opinion, a sling is not entirely necessary. The 2008 Men's Olympic Gold Medalist won his gold medal without one. Even so, some kind of sling can greatly aid training.

Types of Slings The common slings in use are: finger slings, wrist slings, and bow slings. Finger slings attach to the archer's thumb and first finger on her bowhand (*see photo*). Finger slings can be purchased but they also can be made easily from something as simple as a shoestring (*see*

> www.youtube.com/watch?v=oX0iNyXdis0 *or*
> www.youtube.com/watch?v=2aaO7ECp9Ow).

Wrist slings attach to the bow wrist and then wrap around the bow and reattach to the sling at the wrist. Recurve archers prefer finger slings and secondarily wrist strings. Bow slings attach to the bow with the archer inserting her wrist through the sling before gripping the bow. Bow slings are preferred by compound archers and for beginning archery class bows. Traditional archers often shoot without a sling.

How Do I Know My Athlete Is Ready for a Sling?

If an archer is exhibiting a tendency to grasp the bow strongly or to grab at it after each shot, a sling might help in curing these form problems.

How to Get Started (Sling)

Basic Setup Once the style of sling is chosen, it must be fitted so it is the correct length. Shoestring finger slings are preferred as the length of the sling can be adjusted by adjusting the size of the loop one begins with. There needs to be 1.5″-2″ slack between the sling and the bow handle when the bow hand is in proper position (*see photo bottom right*). Wrist slings are similarly adjusted. Bow slings need to be slack enough that the sling exerts no force on the archer's wrist at full draw.

Training (Sling)

Initial Stages Once the sling is in place and your archer is ready to shoot, ask them to hold the bow at arm's length and drop it. The sling will catch the bow. This exercise will prove to the archer's subconscious mind that they no longer have to fear dropping their bow.

Then have the archer shoot some shots close up with his eyes closed. Have him focus on the feel of the bow jumping out of his bow hand and the sling catching it. Transition to shooting at targets with the sling but still focusing on the feel of the bow leaving a relaxed bow hand.

Later Stages It should only take a few weeks of shooting for the sling to feel normal.

Potential Pitfalls (Slings)

1. *Once a Sling is Adopted, Forgetting to Put It On Can Be Embarrassing*

Occasionally at a competition a young archer forgets to put on his sling and his bow goes flying out in front of the shooting line. All of the archers laugh (the source of the potential embarrassment), but all of the coaches are saying "Yes!" quietly to themselves. That is the reaction of a bow being shot correctly.

2. *Commercial Slings aren't Necessarily Easy to Adjust*

Commercial finger slings often are not sold in various lengths and cannot be adjusted. Most wrist slings can be adjusted by tying knots (either in new positions or to make the length of the sling shorter. Most bow slings are designed to be adjusted.

Photo by Andy Macdonald

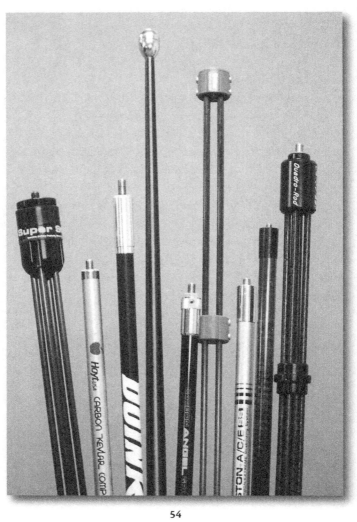

5
How To . . .
Introduce Stabilizers

General Background Information

Commercial stabilizers were first used in the 1960s and have become almost universally popular. By spreading the weight of the bow out, the bow becomes harder to move, especially in the critical 10-20 millisecond portion of the shot as the arrow leaves the bow and the bow is being held one-handed. Modern stabilizer systems not only steady the bow but are also designed to absorb vibrations left over from the shot. The arrow carries away only about 75-80% of the energy put into the bow and much of the rest is released as vibration. If the bow arm and bow shoulder absorb all of that vibration, they will fatigue faster and possibly suffer injury in the long term.

Types of Stabilizers Many archers use long rod stabilizers (*see photo left*). Olympic Recurve archers prefer a long rod with V-bar and twin side rods. Some compound archers use a long rod and a single side ride to balance the weight of compound bow sights which are rather heavy. Compound archers who shoot in "hunting styles" may be limited to a short stabilizer (<12″).

Archers using long rods find that their bows roll forward after release. This bias to roll forward makes movement in any other direction more difficult and helps make the archer more consistent.

Photo by Andy Macdonald

How Do I Know My Athlete Is Ready for a Stabilizer?

Once an archer has good basic form and has been taught a basic aiming system, such as point of aim, a stabilizer can be introduced.

How to Get Started (Stabilizer)

Basic Setup Both short and long rod stabilizers are merely screwed into the boss in front of the bow. A great many different lengths are available. To determine an approximate reasonable length for a long rod have the archer hold their bow at their side, back facing down (string up). Have them bend their arm slightly, then measure from the back of the bow to the ground.

Most long rod stabilizers have "tip weights" that can be attached via threads onto the tip of the stabilizers. Beginning stabilizer users should use minimal tip weights or no tip weight at all (lightweight plastic end caps are available for many).

A *Potential Pitfall* A pitfall to avoid when introducing stabilizers is creating a bow with too much mass. Compound bows are particularly heavy and if your student is young or has little upper body development, she may struggle holding up such a heavy

Not only does a long rod make a handy prop so you don't have to carry your bow while waiting but this position shows you about how long of a rod is needed (see text).

bow. Adding even more weight in the form of tip weights exacerbates this error.

Training (Stabilizer)
Initial Stages Archer's who have become used to their bare bow rocking backward in their hand during their followthrough may find the bow taking a more neutral position (no rocking), or in the case of the long rod, having the bow roll forward.

Start by having your archer explore the new followthrough dynamics while shooting blank bale. Have them observe their bow's new tendencies. If they have been introduced to a bow sling, be sure they wear it.

Transition to shooting at targets with the stabilizer, still focusing on the feel of the bow leaving a relaxed bow hand.

Later Stages It should only take a few weeks of shooting for the stabilizer to feel normal. Often the bow's dynamics are changed sufficiently to need new sight

Photo by Lloyd Brown

marks. You may want to experiment with how smaller and larger tip weights affect the feel of the shot.

Potential Pitfalls (Stabilizer)

1. *Avoid Adding Weight to an Already Too Heavy Bow*

Especially for young compound archers, adding accessories to their bows may be limited by their ability to hold that much weight up at arms' length. Watch for signs your archer is struggling during the followthrough with the weight of the bow. Installing accessories like stabilizers may have to be put off or the archer may need to do exercises to build up their deltoid muscles (on both sides).

2. *Adding a Stabilizer Will Cause Some Accidents*

Adding a rod sticking out a couple of feet in front of the bow may cause archers to accidently whack other archers and themselves with this new piece of equipment. Caution your students to be careful of this but also indicate that it is common; all that is required is an apology and over time your archer will become used to it.

6
How To . . .
Introduce Bow Sights

General Background Information

Bow sights ("sights" in the vernacular) have been around for a hundred years or so. The first were rather primitive but today's sights include an incredible array of features and adjustments (both being potential sources of confusion). For our purposes we will separate all sights into two categories: *target sights* and *pin sights*.

Target sights have a single moveable aperture (the

thing lined up with the point of aim) whereas pin sights have a number of "pins" (typically 1-6) set in fixed positions associated with targets at fixed distances. Targets at distances other than those the pins are set for must be estimated according to where one or more of those pins should be placed (*see illustrations*).

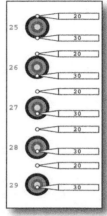

How Do I Know My Athlete Is Ready for a Bow Sight?

This is somewhat complex. Some students start with sights on their bow but this is not preferred. It is better to start all beginners with a "bare" bow using what is called "instinctive aiming."

One must "read" between the pins. In this example see how the 20 and 30 yard pins are used at the various yardages.

This term is actually a misnomer; it should be "learned aiming" or some such. In any case, just instruct students to "look at the spot you want to hit" which is typically target center. The advantage of this is that *if* (and it is a big if) they can get their minds out of the way, the simple desire to have the arrows land in the center will trigger subconscious processes that will result in arrows in the center.

Once a student can shoot reasonably sized groups (at short distances) teach them to shoot using a point of aim (POA) system. "Consistently good groups" are important because these show that the student has somewhat good basic archery form and execution. By adding POA aiming they can learn a great deal about the process of aiming without the expense or the fiddling around required to learn to use a sight.

Once POA comes naturally, introduce a sight if the archer desires one.

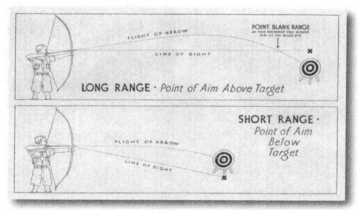

How to Get Started (Bow Sight)

Basic Setup The sight can be as simple as a piece of foam tape with a hat pin in it or as elaborate as a full-blown target sight or pin sight. Have them mount their sight and set it up according to the manufacturer's instructions. Much can go wrong here. If the sight bar or pin stack is not parallel to the string, windage will change with each elevation change (*see the sidebar* "How Far Out Should the Sight Be Placed?"). Similarly the aperture/pin stack needs to be in the plane of the bowstring. If these issues aren't taken care of during setup, difficulties in learning are sure to ensue.

Do not introduce a peep sight (if desired, compound only) at the same time as the sight itself. Your student has been shooting without a peep and can continue to do so when a sight is introduced. A peep sight can be added later. By breaking things down into "doable" chunks you create a ladder of success and also show students some of the various ways arrows are shot from bows.

Training (Bow Sight)

A piece of foam tape with a pin stuck into it sideways can make a bowsight good enough to learn on.

Initial Stages With the sight in place on your student's bow, have them shoot "off the point" (i. e. the way they have been) at a fairly close target confirming that their point of aim is correct. After several shots that way, ask them to look at the position of the sight's aperture pin is while they are at their POA, and have them take several more shots. Next ask them to move the aperture pin until it shows up at target center when they are "on point," and have them take several more shots. Then ask the student "Could you use the sight aperture/pin in place of the arrow point to aim with?" Finally have them use the aperture to aim with while taking several more shots.

In this fashion you establish, in short order, that the sight aperture and the arrow point are equivalent aiming devices. This may sound laborious, but it goes very smoothly and quickly. And having point of aim in their skill set allows them to adapt to "aiming off" to adjust for wind with no qualms.

Then go on to teach "sighting in."

Note In a class situation, we don't teach sights unless

the archers own them.

The advantage of this process is that students can go back to aiming off the point and still shoot well, and that it emphasizes the actual role of the sight, which is simply to position the bow so that if a shot is well executed, the arrow goes into the center. It also allows the student to focus on becoming reliably repeatable in his/her shots before becoming significantly focused on aiming. (Even so, when sights are introduced, there is some initial degradation of group sizes; see below.)

Potential Pitfalls (Bow Sight)

1. *Initial Degradation of Form and Execution*

The focus on the aiming process can distract from the other factors necessary to execute good shots. This is expected, but as your archer gets acclimated, they need to return to normal levels of focus while aiming. This will show up as the archer's shot timing returns to normal.

2. *Initial Degradation of Group Sizes*

Of course, this is related to #1 above. The form degradations may be very small and only show up as an expansion in group sizes. The groups getting smaller than before the sight was introduced is a sign that good form has been recovered and greater consistency has been achieved.

How Far Out Should the Sight Be Placed?

The simple answer to this question is "you can put it anywhere." The first sights were, like the foam tape sight, affixed to the back or the belly of the bow. Only much later did someone get the idea to extend the sight away from the bow (both for target and pin sights).

Aperture goes in here —

Knob can be loosened and the extension bar slid back and forth.

There are a number of parameters involved as to what the best sight extension might be, some may not affect all sight designs.

1. The farther out the sight bar is extended, the farther apart the sight marks or pins are. At longer distances, this means the aperture/lowest pin can get in the way of your arrow. At shorter distances some interference with the archer's sight line from the riser may occur (especially if the riser is short). Youths trying to "make distance" often move their sight bar closer to the riser, even inside

of the riser (you just turn it around and insert it into the mount from the other side) to benefit from these tendencies.

2. The farther out the sight bar (and aperture), the more sensitive the sight, allowing you to aim with more precision. (This is the rifle sights being better than pistol sights argument.) On the other hand, the farther out you hold it, the harder it is to hold it steady.

3. If you shoot with a peep sight, the aperture may be moved in and out to make your peep hole concentric with your scope housing (lining up the peep opening with the circular housing of the aperture/scope/pin stack is a form of collimation that makes aiming more precise).

4. With telescopic apertures ("scopes" in the vernacular), it gets complicated. While these apertures are sold by the power (4X, 6X, etc.) the actual magnification is a function of the distance from peep to lens (the greater the separation, the greater the power).

5. The farther out the sight bar, the more forward-heavy your bow will be (which is why you will see some designs have the sight bar at the bow with a long (and lightweight) carbon fiber boom out to the aperture.

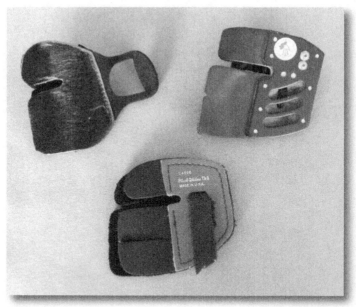

(Top) A three-finger shooting glove (only recommended for hunting).
(Bottom) Three different styles of finger tabs.

7
How To . . .
Introduce Finger Tabs

General Background Information

"Finger protection" goes back many centuries. Modern archers want not only protection from the pressure exerted by the string (which can cause nerve damage if not dealt with) but also a device that allows the string to slip cleanly off of it, as well as a device that can aid in consistent finger placement on the string shot after shot.

Myriad devices have been used for "finger protection" but for our purpose we will break them down into two categories: *shooting gloves* and *shooting tabs*. Shooting gloves consist of either a full glove or a glove with three fingers, possibly with a spiderwork connection system (*see photos*). Shooting tabs ("tabs" in the vernacular) are small patches of materials that usually strap to one or more fingers and may have multiple layers and even metal frames (to help with accurate positioning of fingers of the bowstring and to prevent squirming under the pressure of the bowstring (*see photos*)).

Shooting gloves are usually only worn by traditional archers and then often only traditional bowhunters (a tab can be dropped and lost, whereasa glove is attached to your hand). The topic here is primarily target archery and since target archers almost exclusively use tabs, tabs will be the focus.

How Do I Know My Athlete Is Ready for a Finger Tab?

In beginner classes archers often go without a tab as the ones supplied are clumsy and not much help; only when students experience some finger sensitivity are they supplied with tabs. In other classes, tabs are issued to all archers.

Archers are ready for a tab right from the beginning or when they request one.

How to Get Started (Finger Tab)

Basic Setup Tabs must fit; *how* depends on whether the archer is shooting "split finger" (one finger above the arrow and two below) or "three-fingers under" (three fingers under the arrow). Tabs for three-fingers under shooting need to be slightly taller than the three fingers the archer puts on the string. This is because the string wraps around both the top and bottom fingers at full draw and protection is needed there. Tabs for split-finger archers need to be slightly taller than those same three fingers but with an arrow between the top two (a pencil may be substituted for measurement or fitting). A slightly too large tab can be trimmed, but a slightly too small tab is just too small.

Tabs need to be "broken in" by shooting with them. Serious archers should buy two at a time and shoot them in alteration (day by day) so they will have a backup tab (in case one gets lost) at the same stage of wear. When tabs seem to be getting worn out, two new ones need to be purchased and broken in during practice while there is still some life in the first two.

Training (Finger Tab)

Initial Stages Training simply involves shooting with the tab, properly worn. The tab should be tightly secured to the string fingers so that it does not squirm around. The fingers need to be relaxed but together. If the fingers are splayed out on one shot and tightly together on the next, the results will be different.

Beginners need to take extra time while "setting hands" to make sure the tab is properly placed on the string. The fingers need to be together with the string in or slightly behind the first groove in from the finger tips (this is called a "deep hook").

Later Stages After some use, the tab's top surface should show a single indentation, made by the pressure of the string. If the indentation is hourglass-shaped, the string hand is being put on the string at different angles. If the indentation is wide, the position of the string on the fingers is being varied. Coaches should check the student's tab from time to time for these signs of inconsistency.

Metal Bodies and Finger Spacers More advanced tabs often come with metal bodies and/or finger spacers (*see photos at front of chapter*). Since the metal body acts as a clamp for the tab's flexible materials (leather, natural or synthetic, being the most common) the frame tends to be the same height is the leathers. Fitting should be done as above but also check to see that the metal frame fits in your archer's hand comfortably. It is not unusual for young archers to forego metal tabs until they reach adulthood, opting instead for a high quality soft tab like the Wilson Brothers *Black Widow* tab (*see photo at front of chapter—bottom*).

There is still some debate about the use of finger spacers (for those shooting split-finger) but the vast majority of finger shooters use them. These can be modified with tape, moleskin, files, grinders, or whatever to make the shape compatible with the archer's hand and to prevent calluses from the fingers rubbing against the spacer.

Potential Pitfalls (Finger Tab)

1. *Squeezing the Finger Spacer*
Some archers acquire the habit of squeezing the finger spacer between their top two fingers trying to keep the hand in the same place on the tab. This increases tension in those fingers and makes it harder for the string to flick them out of the way during the release. The fingers need to be together but very, very gently.

2. *Too Small or Too Large Tabs*
This often occurs to youths who may be using hand-me-down or second hand equipment. If the tab is too small, too little protection is offered and calluses may develop or pain may result. If the tab is too large, it may interfere with getting a clean loose of the string. This is the first

piece of archery equipment a beginning archer should buy and a quality tab can be had for around $10. They just need to make sure it fits.

The hole in the peep sight is lined up around the housing of the aperture giving perfect collimation for perfect aiming.

8
How To ...
Introduce Peep Sights

General Background Information

Peep sights are a relatively new innovation. They are small lozenges with angled holes through them. They are inserted into the bowstring and tied in place. When the bow is drawn, the angled hole becomes level with the ground, allowing the archer to look *through* the string (rather than around it) to see their sight's aperture (*see photos*).

Since their inception, the hole has been at a 45° angle but the recent development of very short axle-to-axle compound bows has led to the development of 37° peeps. Purchasers must be aware that there are two types and they need to get the correct one (which is based upon the axle-to-axle length of the bow and the archer's draw length).

The size of the hole through the peep sight determines a lot. One manufacturer has peeps with these hole sizes: ¼″, ⅛″, ³⁄₃₂″, ¹⁄₁₆″, ³⁄₆₄″, and ¹⁄₃₂″. Beginners should start

1/32" 3/64" 1/16" 3/32" 1/8"

with a fairly large hole—⅛″ or ³⁄₃₂″. As they gain experience they may choose differently. If the hole is much too large, it is hard to align it with the housing of the aperture; ditto if it is too small. Additionally, peep holes that are too small are hard to see through in dim light (dim indoor ranges, deep shadows under trees, etc.).

You can buy a brand new peep sight for just a few dollars. Some actually come with a little hood on them to keep the sun off of the inner surface. There is a bowhunting model with a rubber tube to ensure the peep is aligned at full draw. It is not recommended for target archery.

How Do I Know My Athlete Is Ready for a Peep Sight?

Peep sights are used in combination with bow sights on compound bows only (at least in competition). They are not allowed in a great many shooting styles, Olympic Recurve being the foremost.

Peep sights can be introduced any time after the bow sight is introduced. Introducing them simultaneously with a sight makes for a great deal of form and equipment adjustments at one time, something to avoid.

How to Get Started (Peep Sight)

Basic Setup To install the peep, have your archer address a target of middle distance, come to full draw, close their eyes, and settle in. You then place a tiny strip of masking tape onto the bowstring right in front their aiming eye (in line with the aperture). Then have your archer let down the bow. This is the location for the peep to be installed.

Install the peep (a bow press can be used to take the tension off of the bowstring making this much easier) with care that none of the strands of the bowstring get damaged. To test the position, have your archer draw their bow as before but with their eyes closed from the beginning; once settled in at full draw, have them open their aiming eye. He should be looking right through the peep (although possibly not at his aperture or target as his eyes were closed the whole time he was drawing). If the peep is not perfectly placed, have him let down and then you can slide the peep slightly up or down to make it perfect. The reason you can only do this slightly is because the bowstring has twists in it and movement of any great extent will also result in the peep being rotated along the twisted string, thus making it impossible to see through. If the peep is at the right height but is rotated out of position, either uninstall and re-install or see below for a procedure to rectify this problem.

Do *not* start shooting yet as you will run into a problem, namely the peep will more than likely pop out of the bowstring from the shock and/or vibration of shooting. There are several methods to secure it. The easiest is to simply tie on two nock locators, one above and one below the peep sight. This is done in exactly the same way an ordinary nocking point locator is tied on a bow string. Then slide the two "nock locators" against the peep. The tension from the spread strands will keep the locators in place as well as keep the peep from popping out. This method has the advantage that if the peep needs to be moved slightly, you can just spread the locators, move the peep, and then slide them back. A more secure system can be used when you have the peep exactly where you want it (this involves tying the peep onto the string directly, see the manufacturer's instructions).

More Advanced Setup A key aspect of using the peep is to get the "hole" through the peep to line up with the circular housing of the sight. There needs to be a gap between the two. If there is not, the peep can be swapped for one with a larger or smaller hole or the sight can be extended farther (making the housing appear to be smaller) or less far (making the housing appear to be bigger). Considerable fiddling may be needed until everything is well lined up. Note that extending the sight or changing the size of the peep hole both have other ramifications: on sight marks, for instance, and a peep that is very small is hard to see through in dim light, as mentioned above.

Training (Peep Sight)
Initial Stages Once installed, it is a little hard to ignore, so it will be included in all of the training exercises. A basic rule of practice is to maximize the number of reps of the element being practiced. For peep practice, start

by having your student draw to anchor, checking to see that the inside edge of the peep hole and outside edge of the aperture housing are concentric and then let down. Draw again, repeat the check, and then shoot. If your student's tolerance for boredom is high, have them do two, three, or four or more practice peep alignments before each shot. It will not take too many repetitions to establish this habit. In the shot sequence, checking peep alignment goes between "Find Your Anchor" and "Aim."

Potential Pitfalls (Peep Sight)

1. *The Peep Rotates When the Bow is Drawn (Release Aid)*

This is typically due to a rotating bowstring. When constructed, the bowstring had twists built into it. But if the string stretches, the string also rotates, taking the peep out of line. Some strings are sold already stretched to eliminate this problem. One solution is to use a D-loop. By tying the D-loop on so that it is oriented in the same direction as is the peep, when the bow is drawn the D-loop pulls the peep into proper position. Another is to orient the peep so that when the rotation occurs, the peep ends up in the right place.

2. *The Peep Rotates When the Bow is Drawn (Finger Release)*

In addition to the problems described in #1 (above), finger shooters can also cause the string to rotate as their fingers curl or uncurl around the string as the bow is drawn. The solution here again is to orient the peep so that when the rotation occurs, the peep ends up in the right place.

A Peep Sight Floats the Anchor

Peep sight users don't have a consistent anchor position as do recurve shooters. The reason is that the peep stays in front of the pupil of the aiming eye. So, when the bow is raised compared to the line of sight, the anchor is lowered. Since the peep sight is closer to the anchor than the bow, the change is slight but real.

Consequently, when compound archers set up their bows, if they are shooting primarily indoors, they will place the peep so that their most comfortable anchor is at 18 m/20 yd. Outdoors they will place their peeps so that their most comfortable anchor occurs at a middle distance. Some elite archers place their peeps while aiming closer to their farthest distance with their most comfortable anchor, which means they will be least comfortable at the closest distance. They argue that a competition is often decided by the scores on those longer targets, so having an advantage there is more important.

Emergency Peep Fixes

Sometimes during competition, a string stretches and the peep no longer lines up. To fix the problem, simply slide the nock locators away from the peep. Figure out how the peep has to rotate to get it to work and then take a strand from one side of the peep and swing it over to the other side accordingly:

- If you take a strand from the right side and take it around the front of the peep it will point the peep more to the left.
- If you take a strand from the right side and take it around the back of the peep it will point the peep more to the right.

    If you already have too many strands on the left and not enough on the right:

- If you take a strand from the left side and take it around the front of the peep it will point the peep more to the right.
- If you take a strand from the left side and take it around the back of the peep it will point the peep more to the left.

When you are done slide the locators back up against the peep.

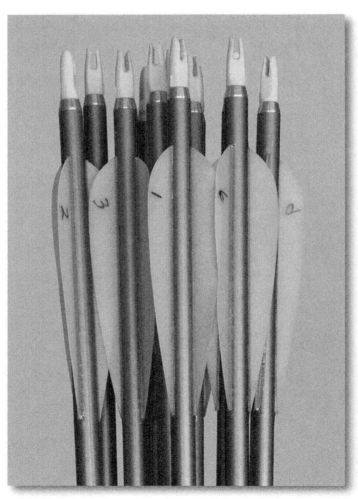

9
How To . . .
Introduce New Arrows

General Background Information

The line of demarcation between beginning archers is when they acquire their own equipment that they can then adjust to their physical attributes. Draw length and draw weight changes occur often when archers are first learning and these can also necessitate new arrows. Also, as archers explore longer shots in target archery, lighter arrows may be necessary to "make distance." And, arrows do suffer wear and do break and do get lost, so at some point more will be needed.

The key criterion when buying arrows is the "spine" of the shafts. The spine is a measure of the resilience, some say stiffness, of the shaft. This must correspond to the magnitude of the forces applied to the arrows. It is important to note that spine ratings are inversely related to arrow shaft stiffness, so heavy drawing bows require arrows of low spine (high stiffness). Light drawing bows require shafts of high spine (low stiffness).

How Do I Know My Athlete Is Ready for New Arrows?

Obviously not having enough arrows to shoot competitive rounds is one sign, but being unable to shoot longer distances can be another (lighter arrows fly farther).

A Potential Pitfall Supportive archery parents often offer to buy equipment for their children in the mistaken notion that this is a form of encouragement. (Equipment that is *earned* is a more supportive approach.) Also, parents often associate "carbon" with higher quality and want to buy carbon limbs, carbon bows, and carbon arrows for their young archer. Unless their child's current performance is adversely affected by their arrows, this is not a good message to send (improvements come through practice, not purchases). An archer must shoot extremely well before the differences between high end arrows and ordinary arrows is apparent. Plus growing children can go through several arrow sizes in just months. We recommend that parents allow their children to earn that higher level gear, when it is appropriate, as a reward for hard work and participation, not as an incentive.

How to Get Started (New Arrows)

Basic Setup Consulting an arrow spine chart is the usual first step. Coaches are expected to give advice as to manufacturer and models as there are a great many available. Just sending students to an archery pro shop may not be enough. Students should not be sent looking for new arrows without a lot of guidance as to what they are looking for.

The arrows need to be purchased uncut. The reason

is that spine charts aren't always as accurate as we would like and whether or not an arrow works for your student depends on quite a number of variables, including nock fit, point weight, shaft length (the primary adjustable factor), shaft spine (the primary unadjustable factor), vane weights, and your archer's form and execution.

Work with a subset of five arrows (you may only want your student to purchase a half dozen arrows until you can confirm a configuration): three are fletched and two unfletched (bare shafts). You begin by doing a bare shaft test (*see sidebar*) to see whether these shafts are too stiff or too weak. Since they are full length and not cut to the archer's draw length (which typically will be shorter) the arrows should test "weak" (cut anything shorter and it becomes harder to bend). After confirming they are actually weak, all five test arrows need to be cut somewhat, nut exactly how much can vary. If the uncut shafts are four inches longer than the archer's measured draw length, cut a full inch off. (If the uncut shafts are only two inches longer than the archer's draw length, you may only want to cut one-half of an inch off.) In any case, another round of bare shaft testing is in order.

The purpose of this procedure is to avoid cutting too much off of the shafts and ending up with unusable arrows. The second bare shaft test should indicate how much stiffness was picked up from the first cut. If the bare shafts are still quite far out on the weak side (but not as weak as they were) you may want to cut another inch or even more off. If the bare shafts have gotten much closer to the fletched shafts, then you want to cut in ever-smaller increments (1″, ½″, ¼″) until the test is exactly as you want it to be.

From that point minor adjustments can still be made in the characteristics of the arrows depending on what you want in the way of characteristics (*see the sidebar* "FOC?")

Fine Points Is your archer still growing? If so, do not ask your student to buy arrows that are intended to be cut to his or her draw length. That draw length can change by as much as an inch in just six weeks. Young archers need "room to grow." Their arrows need to be two or even three inches longer that what is needed now, both for safety (arrows that are or become too short are a safety hazard as they can be pulled off of the arrow rest and onto the back of the archer's bowhand) and growing room. For these arrows to work, they must be chosen to be *one spine group stiffer per extra inch of length.* So, if the arrows are 3″ longer than really necessary and three spine groups stiffer (to compensate for the extra length), if the archer's draw length goes up an inch, his arrows can be cut off an inch (and still be 1″ longer than necessary) but are now stiffer by about the amount needed. Also, if the archer's draw weight goes up by five pounds (more or less) arrows that are one spine group stiffer are needed and a one inch reduction in shaft length provides this.

The extra length and extra shaft stiffness allow for future increases in draw length and draw weight which then need only a small adjustment in shaft length and not entirely new arrows.

Training (New Arrows)

Arrows do not need to be "broken in" or "shot in" but new sight marks are probably necessary (unless the new arrows are identical to the old ones, even so they should be checked).

Potential Pitfalls (New Arrows)

1. *Cutting New Arrows Too Short* (see above)
2. *Buying Shafts That are the Wrong Spine*

This is a major mistake and a costly one. There is no way to "tune" arrows, that is adjust them, to work if they are the wrong spine. Archer parents make this mistake when they "cut down" adult arrows for their children. The arrow lengths are fine but those cuts make them far too stiff to be used well.

The Bare Shaft Test

In bare shaft testing, you need to have two arrows with no fletches. Alternatively you can use several wraps of transparent tape to eliminate the steering ability of your arrow's vanes by taping them down to the shaft.) From about 10-15 yards shoot arrows until you are warmed up and so you can get a good group of three arrows in the center of a target. Then shoot the two bare shafts. (You shoot the second to tell if you shot a good shot with the first bare shaft; they should hit close together!) When the three fletched and two bare arrows form groups, this is what you can learn:

- If the bare shafts strike the target above the fletched group, your nocking point is too low.
- If the bare shafts strike the target below the fletched group, your nocking point is too high. (Always adjust for these first.)
- If the bare shafts strike the target to the left of the fletched group, your shafts are too stiff (RH archer).
- If the bare shafts strike the target to the right of the fletched group, your shafts are too weak (RH archer).

The left and right bare shaft indications are reversed if you are left-handed. And the farther out the bare shafts are, the bigger the problem. Just a couple of inches of separation between the group of bare shafts and the fletched shafts indicates a pretty good test.

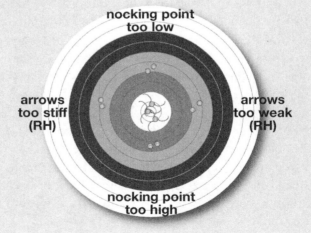

FOC?

In arrow discussions you will hear the term "F-O-C" for "front of center." This is an indicator of weight distribution or balance in arrows. High FOC arrows are quite front heavy; low FOC arrows are not so front heavy. To work at all arrows need to be somewhat front heavy. Someone created arrows that had heavier rears than fronts and these arrows turned end-for-end in mid-flight!

To determine percent FOC all you need to do is balance an arrow on your finger and mark the shaft. Then measure the arrow's full length and find the exact half-way point. The degree the arrow's point of balance is in front of the center is then:

%FOC = (distance from center to balance point/length of arrow) x 100

Target archers shooting long distances want roughly 13-14% FOC. Field archers usually prefer their arrows to be 8-9% FOC. This helps to select the weight of the arrow points.

To get to a higher FOC, first try a slightly heavier point. To get to a lower FOC, try a slightly (con't) lighter point. A more expensive approach is to use heavier or lighter shafts but this is rarely done.

Steve Ruis

How To's . . .

Form
and
Execution

A useful drill to help students connect with the motions in their backs is to have them simulate drawing their bow while laying on their backs. This should be done on a hard floor or a rug, not on grass.

10
How To . . .
Teach the Use of
Back Tension

General Background Information

A bow can be drawn using arm and shoulder muscles or it can be drawn shifting much of the load onto back muscles. The technique using back muscles makes better use of leverage and by using muscles not contained in the draw arm, makes the draw arm less tense allowing it to execute the release of the string better. Additionally, the back muscles are stronger than those in the arm and shoulder, allowing more draw weight to be mastered comfortably.

To the contrary, there are elite level compound archers who are "arm shooters," meaning they do not rely primarily on back muscles while shooting. They can do this because the force needed to hold a compound bow fully drawn is a small fraction of the peak draw force (draw weight) unlike recurve bows and longbows which have peak weight at full draw. The vast majority of elite recurve bow archers use their backs primarily.

How Do I Know My Athlete Is Ready to be Taught Shooting with Back Tension?

If your archer is not just a recreational archer looking to only shoot for fun, the time is now. Any serious recreational archer and all competitive archers should use their backs to draw and hold the bow as much as is possible.

How to Get Started (Back Tension)

Basic Explanation Some youths don't need an explanation but most adults prefer one. If an explanation is wanted, show your student how the draw shoulder is pulled around dragging the draw arm with it, using middle upper back muscles (mostly the *rhomboids*). As the shoulder is rotated around, the elbow is swung along a slightly downward arc. Having the draw elbow at least as high as the archer's chin at the beginning of the draw prevents the draw arm's *biceps* muscles being used and encourages the use of the appropriate back muscles (but doesn't require them).

By placing a fingertip on the tip of each of the archer's *scapulae* (shoulder blades), you can show your archer that the *scapulae* end up pinched up against the spine at full draw. This compression in the back has come to be known as "back tension." If more is needed, have your student lie on their back, on a clean floor or rug. Have them mime drawing the bow (*see photo back two pages*). They should feel their scapulae moving against the floor. (Don't do this on grass as it leaves ter-rific grass stains.)

Another drill is to adopt T-form with both arms in the same position they would be if they were both draw arms, then try to swing both elbows back and around (as if to get them to touch behind the archer's back). Emphasize recognizing the feel in the upper back muscles.

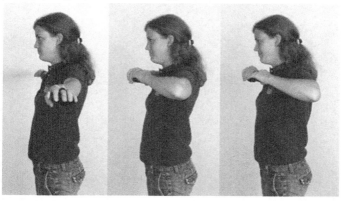

Training (Back Tension)

Initial Stages Using a very light drawing bow (even a 10# recurve bow) can be helpful in getting your student to understand the role of the back while shooting. This is done up close, blank bale, and can be done with eyes closed (to accentuate feeling the moving back muscles). The coach has to watch the student's back to see that the *scapulae* are moving. It helps if the student wears a tight fitting shirt (or pulls the cloth around to the front so it is tight in back). Again, the coach can reinforce the sensa-tion by placing a fingertip on the tip of each scapula.

Later Stages There are more aspects to this technique

performed by elite archers. These are not necessary for a student to learn back tension and may be considered fine points that can be learned later.

Potential Pitfalls (Back Tension)
None

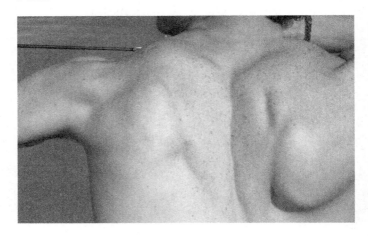

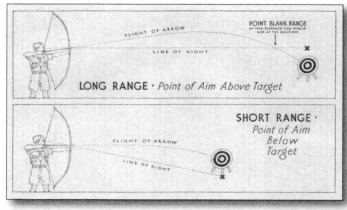

This diagram, from a 1930's pamphlet, explains the point of aim system. To position the bow for a good shot, one lines up the arrow point with a reference mark. Each distance has its own reference mark or "point of aim."

11
How To...
Teach Shooting
Off of the Point

General Background Information
This aiming technique, point of aim or POA shooting, was invented in the Western archery tradition in the mid-1850's and led to very large increases in scores. It is an excellent first aiming technique to teach beginners as it requires no additional equipment to be added, can correct for mismatched equipment, and builds a foundation for later should the archer choose to use a bow sight.

How Do I Know My Athlete Is Ready
to Learn to Shoot off of the Point?
Basic solid archery form and execution are all that are required. This is indicated by your archer shooting consistently good groups at even short distances.

How to Get Started (Shooting Off of the Point)

Basic Introduction Once an archer groups fairly well, indicating they have consistent basic archery form, point of aim technique can be introduced as a first aiming system. For those who want an explanation, once an archer's form becomes consistent, the only significant difference between shots is where they hold their bow. By lining up some part of the bow with some part of the visible background, a consistent aim can be had. The key is to align the bow with the background so that the arrow lands in the desired spot. Any part of the bow can be used for this purpose, but most people use the point of the arrow.

Demonstration Script

Standing 5-7 yards/meters from a large target, aim dead center at the target face by lining the arrow up with target center and loose. The arrow will hit off center, typically quite high. Say "*I just aimed by lining up my arrow point with the target's center, and I missed. Can you figure out where the arrow needs to be aimed to hit in the center?*" Most archers can figure it out. If the arrow hit in the black at 11 o'clock, for example, the next arrow needs to be aimed in the black at 5 o'clock. In any case, say "*the point of aim (POA) can be found by drawing a straight line from tthe point of impact through target center and out the other side exactly as far as the first arrow hit.*" Explain the target clock (*see sidebar*) and then tell your student "*You can use the target face and the target clock to figure out their POA, and then create a mental note, e.g. '5 o'clock in the black' or '5 o'clock in the three ring' to help you visualize where to put your arrow point.*"

Repeat the demonstration, this time aiming at the correct POA. The arrow will hit much closer to the center. *Note* If you are using program equipment or other equipment not fitted to you or if your first shot is not of high quality, this demonstration will not be perfect.

Allow your student to do the same experiment you demonstrated and then ask them to shoot for several shots using their new-found POA. Explain that if their "ranging shot" wasn't perfect, then their POA won't be either, so it is okay to adjust their POA to make it better.

Training (Shooting Off of the Point)

Initial Stages After some practice ask your student to move four or five steps back from the target and shoot using the same POA. The arrows will hit lower. Ask them what they need to do get their arrows back in center. Have them experiment to find their new point of aim.

After several shots repeat this procedure.

When their POA becomes level with target center, they have reached their "point-on-target" distance ("point-on" in today's archery vernacular). At all farther distances than the "point on," the POA will be higher than target center, and at all closer distances it will lower.

A Potential Pitfall Many archers find themselves focusing so much on aiming they lose track of their good archery form. If this happens, have your archer shoot some shots blank bale with their eyes closed (also called blind bale) correcting their form or execution until they are back where they were. This is a normal occurrence. Expect most archers to have form breakdowns as they are learning to aim. Let them know this is normal, as is the time spent "finding their shot" again.

Later Stages After some further practice set up shots that require points of aim off of the target face itself. For longer shots if the target has a wind flag, the top, bottom, and middle of the pennant can be used as can the top, bottom, and middle of the shaft between the pennant and the target butt. Above that twigs or branches in trees or bushes can be used.

For very close shots clumps of grass, dandelions, etc. can be used as POAs. There are a few competitions that allow artificial points of aim, for which archers use tennis or golf balls, ice picks with painted handles, etc.

Some Fine Points

POA Shooting Corrects for Mis-matched Equipment In the introduction to this chapter it was claimed that aiming off of the point can be used to correct for mismatched equipment. This is because if the bow and arrow are tuned to the archer, all POAs should be on a vertical line from 12 o'clock to 6 o'clock through target center. Since arrows that are too stiff tend to fly to the left (for right-handed archers), the POAs can be shifted to the right of the 12 o'clock – 6 o'clock line. Weak arrows tend to fly to the right (for right-handed archers), so the POAs for those arrows will be to the left of the 12 o'clock – 6 o'clock line.

Consequently, if shooting off of the point and the

POAs are on the 12 o'clock – 6 o'clock line through target center, the setup is fairly well-tuned to the archer!

POA Shooting Enhances Good Form Using the arrow point instead of some fixed part of the bow gives very sensitive feedback on an archer's draw length. If an archer over draws her bow, the arrow will tend to go high for that reason but the overdrawn arrow will also make the arrow point move down in the archer's sight picture (because the back end of the arrow is lower than the archer's aiming eye). This also causes the arrow to go higher because the archer will have to raise the too low arrow point farther up to get to her POA. This is a double whammy causing the arrow to go high. A similar situation is created when the archer draws short; both effects cause the arrow to go low.

This sensitivity to draw length consistency will probably never be noticed by your archers, but subconsciously they will make corrections resulting in more consistent draw lengths based on their desire for their arrows to group in the middle of the target.

POA Shooting Prepares for Bow Sight Technique Later, if your archer adopts a bow sight, they will simply center the aperture on the target and use the same point of aim, *i.e.* dead center for each shot. This is true as long as the wind isn't blowing. If a sideways wind is blowing from left to right on the target and pushing good shots out of the center six to eight inches, what is the archer to do? The answer is to "aim off" by six to eight inches up wind. This is the same procedure as learned in point of aim shooting. The mental tool using the clock face and target rings still works.

If a pin sight is adopted, it is rare for a shot's distance to be exactly lined up with a pin's distance and "aiming off" is normal. A 50-yard pin can be used for a 48-yard target but the pin must be aligned with a spot below target center.

POA Shooting is Fun and Inexpensive For students who don't have enough money for a bow sight or maybe aren't interested in one, quite high levels of accuracy can be achieved shooting off of the point.

Introducing the Target Clock

Archers use an analog clock face to orient to circular targets (*see illustration*). Points of aim can be according to ring color, *e.g.* "12 o'clock in the black" or by scoring ring value "8 o'clock in the 3-ring."

Potential Pitfalls (Shooting Off of the Point)

1. *Over-focusing on Aiming Can Degrade Form* (*see above*)

Why Aiming Down the Shaft Doesn't Work

Every beginning archer goes through a couple of stages. First they do as instructed and shoot fairly well, fairly quickly. Then their minds start "trying" to figure out "how to do this" and one of the first things they try is "aiming down the shaft" (also called "shot gunning"). At very close distances this does work but out past ten yards it fails quite miserably.

This is how shotguns are aimed (to some extent) but the velocity of a firearm projectile is tremendously higher so gravity has much less of an effect. Once a slower and heavier arrow leaves the bow it also leaves the archer's line of sight falling at quite a clip, so arrows aimed on center will hit low.

In addition, to get the arrow up to the aiming eye, the rear end of the arrow gets raised which makes the arrow hit even lower. Also, archers tend to tilt their heads to get their aiming eye over the arrow, which degrades the archer's vision. All in all not a good technique.

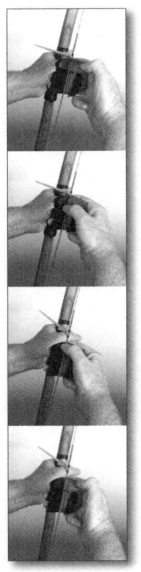

Compound, recurve, and longbow archers can use stringwalking as an aiming technique. This is typically done by running one's thumbnail down from the nock locator, using stitches on the tab or serving wraps as a guide. The tab is then slid down to that point and the shot continues normally. Each distance that corresponds to a shooting distance is called a "crawl." Since no shooting rules allow marks to be put upon bow string, bow, or tab most archers use either the ordinary marks available on some tabs, for example a line of stitches (see photos), or use a center serving material like monofilament serving that will allow them to count down "wraps" of serving.

12

How To . . .
Teach Stringwalking

General Background Information

Stringwalking is said to have been invented less than a century ago, but since archery's history hasn't been codified, this is debatable. Basically stringwalking is gripping the string below the arrow, the lower the string is gripped, the less far the arrow will fly (in effect the arrow is being tilted downward). Target distances can be mapped onto the bowstring quite accurately. Since only a small range of distances can be covered by these "crawls" down the string, various anchors are used for larger ranges. Long distances require low anchors while short distances require high anchors. Some archers also switch between using the arrow point to aim to using other parts of the bow, for example the sight window shelf.

The main advantage of stringwalking over other versions of shooting off of the point is that the same sight picture is used for almost all shots.

Since no shooting rules allow marks to be made on

the bow, bow string, or tab, most archers use either the ordinary marks available on some tabs, for example a line of stitches (*see photos*), or use a center serving material like monofilament serving that will allow them to count down "wraps" of serving. This is typically done by running one's thumbnail down from the nock locator, counting each click or bump along the way. The tab is then slid down to that point (exactly) and the shot continues normally. Each distance down the string corresponds to a shooting distance and is called a "crawl." Some organizations allow these to be written down, while others require them to be memorized. Beginners are urged to take notes so as to minimize mistakes. If their crawls need to be memorized, they can do that later.

Stringwalking is usually only seen in field archery because target archery involves only a few quite long distances (the exception being indoor target archery). Field archery involves shots at many different distances, quite a few of which are at shorter distances.

How Do I Know My Athlete Is Ready to Learn Stringwalking?

This is an option for any student wanting to shoot barebow. Stringwalking is only allowed in a few shooting styles so check to see if your student's "style" is allowed in the competitions they are interested in.

The only preliminary skill needed is the ability to shoot off of the point.

How to Get Started (Stringwalking)

Basic Setup If the archer knows her "point on target" distance (in the vernacular the "point on") that is the best place to start. Have her warm up until she is grouping nicely. Then take five paces closer to the target and have her shoot using the same crawl (zero because of the three-fingers under string grip). The arrow should hit high. Then ask her to stick the tip of her draw hand thumbnail into the string about a quarter inch down from where the tab is touching the arrow and then slide her tab down until the upper edge of the tab is lined up with the point her thumbnail is touching the string. Then the bow is drawn and the shot taken with the same point of aim but using this crawl. The arrow should hit lower.

If the arrow didn't hit in target center adjust the crawl distance: if it needs to hit lower a larger crawl is in order; if higher, a smaller crawl. Once a crawl that works is found, the distance and a description of the crawl are written in the student's notebook. The crawl is described either as a number of wraps of center serving or number of stitches (and fractions thereof) on the archer's tab.

This process is repeated until a number of crawl/distances are mapped.

Advanced Setup Once a number of crawls are determined, work with your archer so they can see that the crawls are linear. For example, if a one stitch crawl equates to four yards closer than the archer's point-on, a two-stitch crawl will be eight yards, a three-stitch crawl 12 yards, etc. Since the crawls are linear, the archer can interpolate between them. Using the previous example, since a one-stitch crawl was 4 yards inside of the archers point-on and a two stitch crawl was 8 yards inside her point-on, a one-and-a-half-stitch crawl (halfway between the one-stitch and two-stitch crawls) should be 6 yards inside of their point-on.

Crawls are limited to about three inches or so down the string as drawing the string this way detunes the bow.

Going Farther Go back to your archer's "point on" distance. This time walk *back* five paces and shoot the same crawl (zero). This time the arrow will hit low. It should be obvious that crawling will not solve this problem as a crawl will cause the arrow to hit the target even lower. (If it is not obvious, let your student puzzle it out.) Instead, archers can choose to "aim off" here. If the arrow landed at 6 o'clock in the blue, they could aim at 12 o'clock in the blue to compensate, but as they continue to move farther from the target soon they would be off of the target completely. A better solution is needed.

That solution is a lower anchor. Most string walkers get by with a high anchor (index finger in the corner of the mouth) and a low anchor (Olympic-style anchor) but some use other variants (middle finger in the corner of the mouth for very short shots, etc.). Each anchor has it's own "point on" target distance and a set of crawls for distances down from there.

Training (Stringwalking)
Initial Stages New anchors have to be trained in. All are best addressed blank bale. Coaches need to give feedback so a good start can be had (*see* "How to . . . Introduce Different Anchors").

Be aware that clickers can be used in training, even

though they are often not allowed in competition or are just impractical (when stringwalking the distance the arrow is drawn varies with the crawl). New anchors are best trained in with a zero crawl.

Later Stages After some practice with a new anchor, the archer's point-on target distance with this crawl has to be found, along with all of the crawls inside that "point on." Notes are taken so each set of crawls and their distances can be compared.

Fine Points When a complete set of crawls for both anchors is available, check to see if the two sets of distances overlap (five or so, from which the others can be figured). If they do, your archer has all distances covered from her low anchor point on to her high anchor biggest crawl. If there is a small gap between the two sets of distances, then the aiming off technique discussed prior using the high anchor/ no crawl setup may fill that gap.

Advanced Training (Stringwalking)

Archers are oriented to target center but at farther distances with smaller aiming rings, and the arrow point can cover the entire aiming dot. Consequently string walkers have adopted a slightly different target picture. They line up the *top* of the arrow point with the *bottom* of the central aiming ring creating a kind of "figure eight" (*see illustration*). This creates a very fine position for aiming. Additional rings below the center can also be used as alignment points as can rings above the center but, since the curved lines go the same way, it is harder to get an exact positioning of the arrow point.

An Alternative to the Low Anchor Some archers

struggle with the low anchor or the low anchor doesn't give enough distance. In this case an option is to "shoot off of the shelf." This involves positioning the target's central scoring ring so that it touches the outside of the arrow and the top of the bow's arrow shelf. This provides a great deal more distance as it raises the bow significantly, but it also aims the arrow off to the right of the target (the target center used to be right on top of the arrow now it is to the left). This is compensated for by either aiming off or moving the string in the archer's string picture quite a bit to the right (how far must be determined by experiment—*see the sidebar* "String Picture and Windage"). All variations must be trained in with repetition.

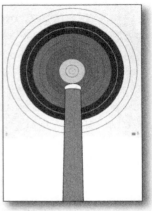

For the most accurate aiming possible, the top of the round arrow point is aligned to the bottom of the center aiming circle, creating a figure "8" shape. This alignment is used on almost all shots.

Potential Pitfalls (Stringwalking)
1. *Available Crawls Do Not Cover Competitive Distances*

Sometimes archers can't seem to cover all of the distances they need to shoot with the anchors and crawls they can master.

Consequently different equipment parameters are needed. Typically these involve more draw weight (which gives higher arrows speeds and more "cast" or distance) and/or lighter arrows (which does the same).

String Picture and Windage

Most beginning archers are unaware that their bow string can be seen at full draw through their aiming eye. Careful positioning of the image of the bow string against the background of the shot can add consistency to an archer's shot. (Compound archers using a peep sight do not have to bother with this as they can look through a peep hole straight through the string.)

To help your archers explore their "string pictures" and the effects of "string alignment," have them play with it using a very light drawing bow at very short distances. Some archers line up the string with their arrow point (not a good idea if you are using the point to aim with). Others use the inside edge of the riser, or the outside edge, etc. What someone uses depends on the shape of their face and the kind of 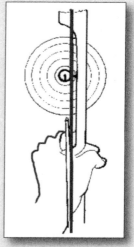 anchor they employ. A different string alignment may be needed for each anchor. When "shooting of the shelf" a right-handed archer may have to move his string in his sight picture a couple of inches to the right.

13
How To . . .
Introduce Different Anchors

General Background Information

Beginners are most often taught an "index fingertip in the corner-of-the-mouth" high anchor position for their string hand but are usually not told why. If asked most coaches say that the "high anchor" is the easiest to teach or to learn, but that is not the reason (and, I believe, untrue). The real reason is that archers begin shooting at very close targets (5-10 yards/meters). At such distances, with a low anchor and the instruction of "look at what you wish to hit" there would be a great many arrows flying over the tops of the target butts. Later, when they have "graduated" to using a POA system, it is more likely to provide a point of aim near target center at short distances.

Various anchors have been used for centuries: to deal with the distances of the York Round, which reach 100 yards, a gentleman in the 1930's stitched a button to his vest to draw to. Archers have drawn to their ears, to their eyes, to their chests, under their chins, to their cheeks, etc. Modern archers use a small subset of these. Typical anchors are the "corner-of-the-mouth high anchor," and the "low or Olympic anchor." The corner-of-the-mouth high anchor involves the tip of the index finger being

High Anchor

Low Anchor

tucked into the corner of the mouth (a common variant being the tip of the middle finger being tucked the same way). The hand is pressed tightly against the face in this position. The "low anchor" involves the hand being pressed up under the jaw with the string being either centered on the chin or at the corner of the chin. The "center anchor" is rarely used as it requires an unusual combination of chin and nose lengths to be used without excessive head tilt.

The purpose of all of these anchors is to *get the string in front of the aiming eye* with the arrow nock a repeatable distance below the aiming eye (vertically). In these positions the arrow's windage is lined up exactly with whatever the archer is looking at. And with the nock lower than the line of sight of the aiming eye, the arrow is set for its parabolic trajectory, arcing first up above the line of sight and then down to it again.

How Do I Know My Athlete Is Ready
for a Different Anchor?

The most common reason students need a different anchor is to "make distance." As mentioned above, since archers start shooting at quite short distances a higher anchor is needed, both to make those shots feel correct and to facilitate POA aiming by providing points of aim very near target center.

But when the targets are moved back, beginners with light drawing bows, heavy arrows, and high anchors need to tilt their shots so far up that it gets difficult to maintain good form. Instead of holding the bow and the front of the arrow higher, a better option is to hold the back of the arrow lower.

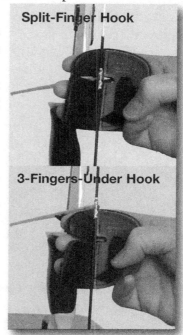

Split-Finger Hook

3-Fingers-Under Hook

The most common ways of doing this are to (a) change from a "three-fingers-under" string hook to a "split-finger" string hook and (b) move from a "high anchor" to a "low anchor."

A split finger string hook moves the nock end of the arrow down by the width of the archer's top finger without changing anything else. This results in a large effect, causing the archer to hold his bow significantly lower at the same distance. The "three-

117

fingers under" hook is ideal for beginners because even if their string hand gets tense to the point of making a fist, the arrow will not be "pinched off" the rest as it would be if they were started with a split-finger grip. After an archer has shot a hundred or so arrows, they have probably learned to relax their string hands, which is the only preliminary skill needed to learn the split finger hook.

If you don't have a protocol for teaching a basic "finger hook," try this. Ask your student to make a Girl Scout/Cub Scout salute and then "curl your fingers." This gets their thumb out of the way and little finger off of the string until at anchor when they can relax both thumb and little finger.

If going to a split-finger string hook does not provide enough "distance" to your archer's arrows, then the next step is to change to a "low anchor." This also moves the nock end of the arrow down, by approximately the distance between the corner of the mouth and the underside of the chin. This is a huge amount and will create more "distance" than the move to split-finger shooting.

Fine Points If all of these changes don't supply the archer with enough distance, they need to modify their setup using some combination of higher draw weight and/or lighter arrows. There are other factors, but these are the greatest by far.

How to Get Started (Different Anchor)

Basic Setup Explain to your archer what these changes will do, describe and (best) demonstrate them. Start blank bale at very close range and stand in Coaching Position 1 (face-to-face with the archer). From that position you can grasp the bottom half of your archer's riser and move the bow up or down as needed to keep your archer on the bale. Be sure to explain that you will be doing this as surprises at full draw rarely end well.

It is perfectly safe to start with a stretch band or string loop but many archers can make the transition with their bow right away. Use your judgment.

Training (Different Anchor)

Initial Stages Once introduced, the archer needs to practice the new anchor or string hand configuration until it is comfortable.

A Potential Pitfall (Pinching Arrows Off of the Rest) When first shooting "split fingered" it is not uncommon for archers to "pinch the arrow off of the rest." This is caused by the archer pinching the arrow nock tightly between his fingers and then, because of tension, curling his fingers as when making a fist. The arrow will swing away from the bow and off of the rest. Therefore you must carefully monitor the first attempts at shooting split-finger. If the arrow comes off of the rest, you must be there (Coaching Position 1) to first get them to let down and second to relax. Once they relax their string hand there will be no more pinching.

A Potential Pitfall (Floating Their Anchor) When changing anchors there is no memory of where the string hand is to go, so it can end not touching the face at al or drifting off position. This is called having a "floating anchor." The cure is for the archer to press his string hand against the side of his face or up under his chin with some pressure. You can introduce the idea of "string picture," i.e. being able to see the string in his aiming eye and lining it up with some part of his bow (*see the Sidebar* "String Picture and Windage" *in the previous chapter*).

Later Stages After some practice, if arrow groups move to the left (right-handed archer) it is a sign of a floating anchor. If occasional arrows get pinched off the rest it is a sign the string hand is getting tense. Recommend corrections. Most archers adapt fairly quickly to these changes.

Fine Points When the low anchor is taught, the chin must be held higher than when a side anchor is used. (The reason is the string fingers have to be flicked forward and out of the way as the string leaves. If the chin is down the fingers will slide down as well as forward (most jaw lines slope down from back to front), a source of inconsistency. Tell your archer that this is needed and demonstrate it for him.

Potential Pitfalls (Different Anchor)
1. *Pinching Arrows Off of the Rest* (see above)
2. *Floating Their Anchor* (see above)

Archery Coaching How To's

Steve Ruis

14
How To . . .
Teach a Finger release

General Background Information

Most archers begin shooting with their fingers on the string. Some will later move on to a mechanical release aid but, if not, a good loose of the string is a significant asset to a "fingers shooter." Contrary to what some claim, it is possible to teach a good finger release.

The key to having a good finger release is relaxation in the string hand. This appears to conflict with the idea that the fingers are curled around the string *using muscles in the hand* but this is not so. The muscles responsible for curling the fingers are in the upper forearm (mostly the *Flexor digitorum profundus* and the *Flexor digitorum superficialis*). You can show your athlete this by having them grasp their upper forearm while curling and uncurling their fingers. There are drills to encourage relaxation in the hand and wrist (*see below*).

Also important for a clean finger release is having a "deep hook," in which the string is at or slightly behind the first joint of the string fingers. If the string is out on the pads of the fingers a great deal of tension is created to keep it from sliding off. This is unwanted.

How Do I Know My Athlete Is Ready
for Finger Release Training?
Whenever your student experiences frustration with her release, it is time. Both recreational and competitive archers will benefit from this training, the mental aspect alone will help.

How to Get Started (Finger Release Training)
Basic Setup Ensure your student is using a deep hook. If not, demonstrate and have her shoot with a deep hook for several minutes. This may cure any qualms over the quality of her release and, if so, that is enough.

If the release is still awkward, have your student make a hook and, facing her, connect your finger hook to hers. Tell her she is to maintain her hook no matter what. Then shake your hand back and forth, first gently and then slightly more vigorously, and look for her hand, wrist, and arm to become relaxed (you can tell this from her resistance to your movement). Once the whole arm is relaxed, reinforce that only the muscles in the upper forearm need to tensed (to make the hook) and everything else needs to be relaxed.

This then is to be integrated into her shooting form.

Training (Finger Release Training)
Initial Stages If needed, try this short drill involving a recurve bow. The bottom limb tip is rested on the stu-

dent's shoe top; the upper limb is firmly held near its tip with the bow hand. The string is grasped in a deep hook near the limb tip, some pull is applied and then the string is loosed. The goal is for the string hand to be about the same height off of the ground as when shooting with the draw side form as much like as when shooting as possible (*see photo*).

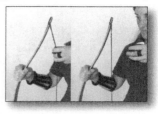

Later Stages After some practice, attention can be shifted to the string hand followthrough. Realize that for all but compound fingers shooters, a live release is recommended. Some coaches make the mistake of teaching the release hand followthrough as *something that is to be done* when it is instead *something that happens as a consequence of other actions.* Teaching a string hand followthrough as a step to be performed will mask any real problems with the release.

The String Hand Followthrough When a shot with a longbow or recurve bow is properly executed, the archer relaxes those muscles in the upper forearm making the hook. No longer being restrained, the bow string flicks the string fingers away and moves towards the bow. If the archer is using back muscles primarily to hold the string at full draw, those muscles will continue to rotate the draw shoulder, bringing the draw hand back along the side of the face, stopping only when the finger tips are under the archer's ear. This happens because the back muscles aren't connected to the arm muscles controlling the hook.

A Potential Pitfall (Soft Shots) Sometimes an archer stops pulling when they have decided to let the string go. This is referred to as "giving up on the shot," or a "soft shot," amongst other things. This will result in no follow through of the string hand and low shots. Your archer must pull through the release with her back muscles.

The Dead Release Because compound fingers shooters have so little draw weight in hand at full draw many of them use a "dead release," which is a release in which the string hand stays put through the release of the string. This has been tried by recurve archers but abandoned as being difficult generally and impossible to do as well as a live release.

Fine Points If you were to ask your archer to assume full draw position (with an arrow on the bow for safety) and ask them to hold as long as they can, they would tell you that it got more and more difficult to hold onto the string. We know, of course, that the holding weight is a function of the bow's design and archer's draw length. It is *constant*, so this feeling (that it is changing or becoming harder to hold) is an illusion. What this illusion that tells us is that the muscles being used to hold the bow are running out of energy. (Doing this exercise for a set number of seconds per repetition as a drill can create

A Dead Release

A Live Release

additional archery fitness that allows for longer holds with greater levels of archer comfort. The British call this drill "Reversals.")

Another illusion that can be useful is the sensation of the string hand *stretching* during the draw and hold. If your archer is not feeling this, they are creating tension to offset it. They should feel as if their hand were stretching (even though it is not). This is a sign that their draw hand is relaxed.

Potential Pitfalls (Finger Release Training)
1. *Soft Shots* (see above)
2. *Indifferent Placement of the Tab on the String*
In order to achieve consistency, the angle the hand makes to the bowstring must be set carefully. A variation here will affect all kinds of other things, including draw length. The tab's top surface should show a single indentation, made by the pressure of the string. As stated in the chapter on finger tabs: if the indentation is hourglass-shaped, the string hand is being put on the string at different angles. If the indentation is wide, the position of the string on the fingers in and out is being varied. Coaches can inspect archer's tabs for feedback on this issue.

A Strong Bow Arm is 60% of the Shot

(Compare the position of her bow arm with the spotting scope behind.)

15
How To...
Develop a
Strong Bow Arm

General Background Information

A common ailment of beginning archers is dropping the bow arm immediately upon release. This is especially common in young compound archers for two reasons: (a) the upper body muscle, including the *deltoid* muscles responsible for holding the bow up, doesn't develop much until late adolescence and (b) compound bows are the heaviest of all of the bows.

A strong bow arm is necessary to developing skill as an archer (*see illustration left*). It has been estimated that it contributes as much as 60% to the success of shots, but this would be very hard to corraborate.

It is important to realize that if your archer hasn't been through puberty, there is little you can do (even weight training isn't much help). If your archer is toward later adolescence, then weight training can help.

If your archer is very young or is older but has a shoulder infirmity, widening his stance will create greater leverage and make it easier to keep the bow arm up. It can be narrowed later.

How Do I Know My Athlete
Needs to Develop a Stronger Bow Arm?

A key indicator of quality shots is the ability to hold the bow up during the followthrough. The inability to do this is a form flaw which is usually called "dropping the bow arm." It is a major cause of low shots.

How to Get Started
(Developing A Stronger Bow Arm)

Basic Drill To acquaint your archer with having a steady bow arm, have them address a blank bale at quite close range. Instead of using their bow sight or other aiming technique, once they are sure their arrow is going to hit the bale, have them sight along one of their bow hand's knuckles by lining it up with some feature on the surface of the bale. The game is to shoot and hold the knuckle in line through and after the shot. This drill might be done for 5-10 minutes at the beginning of each shooting session.

Training (Developing A Stronger Bow Arm)

Basic Approach If weight training is appropriate (it is recommended that weight training be very limited until a youth has gone through puberty.), all you need is a gallon plastic milk container. A gallon of water weighs just over eight pounds and is also eight pints, so each pint of water added to the jug increases the weight one pound. Start your athlete doing side arm raises at home (standing straight, slowly lift the arm sideways until it is level with the shoulder, much like a bow is raised) with one pint of water in the milk jug. Do three sets of ten with each arm every other day. When that exercise is comfortable, add another pint of water. Continue adding water to the jug until the weight simulates the bow's weight (four pints for youths, six pints for adult recurve archers, eight pints for compound archers). This drill can be made more intense by counting to three (or four or five) when the jug is shoulder level and before lowering it for the next repetition.

Potential Pitfalls
(Developing A Stronger Bow Arm)

1. *Young Athletes Can Overdo It (Especially Males)*
Young (typically male) archers tend to be a bit overzealous, especially when it comes to draw weight and heavy bows. Too much draw weight and too much bow weight both inhibit progress learning to shoot well.

2. *Your Competitive Archer May Actually Be a Recreational Archer*
The above drills are quite dull. Competitive archers will be willing to do them but if your archer balks it may be because he is a recreational archer at heart. Recreational archers (our definition) only want to shoot for the fun of it or for social reasons. If your archer resists doing such drills it may be because there is a conflict with their basic motivation, which is *not* a flaw in the archer's character.

Steve Ruis

16
How To . . .
Create a
Good Followthrough

General Background Information

The followthrough is misunderstood. Most coaches explain it by making a comparison with other sports like bowling, baseball, and golf which are really not comparable. Unlike in most other sports, though, the followthrough in archery involves very little to do, but gives an archer feedback on all of the forces acting on the bow and arrow from the moment the release begins, and it is crucial that an archer aspiring to excellence become aware of it and pay attention to what it tells them.

Most beginners are taught to hold their bow arm up (the key and only real instruction) until the arrow hits the target (not a good signal). It is better to tell beginning archers that they need to hold the bow up until their bow "takes a bow." The bow taking a "bow" signals the end of the followthrough in a consistent fashion (unlike the time it takes an arrow to fly to a target which varies with distance). The first feedback a beginning archer gets from their followthrough is that, if they have a relaxed bow hand, the top limb will rock back in the hand during the followthrough (thus taking a "bow").

Additional information comes in the form of the bow bowing consistently. If the bow bows slightly to the left one time and slightly to the right the next, there is bow hand torque involved and the bow hand needs attention. If the bow rocks forward then rocks back, the archer is injecting a high wrist into the shot. If the top limb of the bow snaps backward more quickly than in previous shots, possibly the bow was "heeled" during that shot.

When stabilizer systems are added, both the speed and direction of the bow reaction are changed. Long rod stabilizers generally cause the bow to "bow" forward and many modern compound bows are so heavily reflexed (designed with the grip very close to the bow string) that they are quite front heavy and will bow forward even without a stabilizer.

When stabilizers are used, especially long rods, coaches can learn a great deal by watching the stabilizer tip during shots. Being extended quite far from the bow, the tip amplifies even small movements occurring upon release so they can be seen. Ideally, upon release the tip of a long rod stabilizer should move straight forward (toward the target) an inch or so before the "bow" takes place. If it pops up instead, for example, the archer's center of contact on the grip was probably too low. Coaches need to pay attention to long rod behaviors because of all they can tell us.

How Do I Know My Athlete Is Ready to Create a Good Followthrough?

A good followthrough is learned in stages. Even beginners can benefit from paying attention to their followthrough. Since relaxed hands and good T-form are essential for consistency and accuracy, getting feedback that on these aspects through the shot itself is quite valuable.

More advanced archers need to learn the nuances of how their bow behaves when shot (called the "bow reaction") so they can make necessary corrections from arrow to arrow in competition.

It is quite common, though, for elite compound archers to cut off their followthroughs shortly after release. They do this to reduce wear and tear on their bow shoulders. They can get away from a full followthrough because they have shot tens of thousands of arrows and are finely attuned to the feel of a good shot. This is yet another reason that less advanced archers need to be very careful when emulating elite or pro archers.

Also see "How to . . . Develop a Strong Bow Arm."

How to Get Started
(Creating a Good Followthrough)

Basic Steps Beginners should be taught to look for the bow's "bow" as a sign of a relaxed bow hand and a signal that the shot is over and the bow arm can be relaxed. This will not only improve their shooting but will also establish the followthrough as a form step important to attend to.

Training (Creating a Good Followthrough)

Initial Stages While beginners, barebow archers will benefit by being encouraged to have their bows upper limb rock backward during followthrough. This must be as a consequence of having a relaxed bow hand on the bow, not an action performed. Some students struggle with this and the use of a sling may help them.

To introduce the idea, have your students take a bow one-handed in their best T-form. Have them relax their bow hand: the bow should adopt a neutral position which is at about a 45° angle backward (top limb toward the archer). This is the position the bow should be in at the end of each shot.

A Potential Pitfall Coaches need to watch their archer's followthroughs carefully as some students, seeking perfection, will attempt to guide the bow in its followthrough. This can be noticed in the fact that the bow will rock more slowly than if the archer just lets the bow go where it will. An attempt to control the followthrough destroys any useful information in the bow reaction and replaces it with feedback on how well the followthrough was controlled which is basically useless information.

A *Potential Pitfall* Compound archers using bow slings (a loop attached through the bow through which the archer inserts her wrist—*see photo*) have a somewhat more complicated task. The bowsling will result in their bow hanging from their wrist if the bow is just dropped. Consequently, most compound archers using bow slings will "catch the bow" with the fingers of their bow hand as it rolls forward (*see black arrow in photo below*). It is crucial that the effort to do this come after the arrow is away and that it involve a minimum of movement.

Later Stages Paying attention to the followthrough can be practiced while shooting blind bale (blank bale, eyes closed) and in a drill of "Call Shot." This drill involves shooting at a longer distance; immediately after the shot and followthrough the archer turns to the shooting line and tells you where the arrow hit (you confirm this with a spotting scope or binoculars. The archer can do this drill on her own by putting a video camera on a tripod in your place and speaking to the camera. This drill involves a combination of remembering where her aperture was in her sight picture along with "reading" her followthrough. For example, she may have been centered on the target but her followthrough told her that she dropped her bow arm so she might say "6 o'clock" or "straight low." As another example, she made a good strong shot but her aperture was on the left edge of the target's center, she might say "9 o'clock" or "dead left." Some archers get adept enough at this drill to be able to call their shot quite accurately, *e.g.* "8-ring at 7 o'clock."

Potential Pitfalls
(Creating a Good Followthrough)
1. *Guiding the Followthrough* (see above)
2. *Compound Bow Slings Require Additional Technique* (see above)

17
How To . . .
Create a
Surprise Release
(Compound)

General Background Information

Mechanical release aids have been around for about forty years and, of course, at first they didn't come with instruction manuals. They still don't. Even so, the general consensus among target archers is that they be used in such a way as to achieve a "surprise release." A surprise release is one in which the archer does not know exactly when the release will trigger the shot (even though the release goes off with considerable consistency in the archer's shot cycle). This is the same strategy used by competition rifle shooters who set up their triggers to be "heavy," that is to require quite a large amount of force to get them to set off a shot and also to have a minimum amount of "throw," that is trigger movement. (If the trigger moves over a noticeable distance, one's brain will calibrate that distance and know exactly when the trigger will reach the point at which the shot will occur—so, no "surprise.")

It is recommended that compound archers set their "triggers" up the same way—heavy trigger pressure, minimal throw. If a triggerless release is used, it needs to be set up so the release goes off when the archer reaches perfect alignment and then the archer learns to shoot it that way.

Realize that one does not have to shoot with a surprise release. A number of very successful compound archers do not. Instead, they consciously activate their release aids (so,etimes called "punching" the trigger/release). But for the vast majority of compound target archers, a surprise release is the route to excellent shooting with the least amount of training.

Many bowhunters are very successful swatting/punching their triggers when they want to shoot. This is a totally conscious, non-surprise release. It works as a bowhunting technique because a hunter might have anywhere from zero to two shots per day. If a target archer were to use the same technique, shooting many dozens of shots per day, poor results and probably target panic are in his future.

How Do I Know My Athlete Is Ready to Learn a Surprise Release?

No matter when an archer adopts a mechanical release aid, a surprise release should be taught.

How to Get Started
(Learning a Surprise Release)

See "How to . . . Teach Release Aids." Using a "rope bow" is critical to success. If you start your archer on his bow and an accidental release occurs, you may set him back for weeks or months.

The surprise release is part of a basic release training scheme.

Training (Learning a Surprise Release)

Initial Stages Again, a surprise release is part of a basic release training scheme. After some practice with the rope bow, transition to the archer's bow. Once incorporated into an archer's technique (recreational or competitive) it gets practiced along with all of the other form elements.

Later Stages There are some things that must be monitored as problems can be somewhat difficult to see.

A Potential Pitfall The closer an archer is to being a beginner, the more variable the timing of his shot is. If an archer struggles with shots taking too long he can begin to activate his release more consciously and thus slowly get away from a surprise release. Archers who "punch" their release triggers can do so quite subtly. One way to check this is to video the release for several shots (do not set up the camera so close that it intrudes on the shot— zoom in). What you are looking for is the thumb or finger actuating the release moving more quickly at some point in the process prior to the shot going off and/or more extensive movement of that appendage. (If punching the trigger, the movement is more abrupt, with the appendage on the trigger moving both farther and faster.)

A drill to work though such problems is to have the archer shoot with two or more release aids, set to different speeds. This is a somewhat expensive drill in that two release aids of the same model are recommended, but even using different models can be beneficial.

Potential Pitfalls
(Learning a Surprise Release)
1. *Punching Can Creep In* (see above)

18
How To . . .
Adapt to New Bows

General Background Information

Archers, especially young archers, often acquire new bows. Too often these changes are unplanned in that a bow became available at a good price or the archer followed a whim to "try barebow" or "try compound."

When a new bow is being considered, it is important to make sure that it is fitted to your archer. Bows that are too heavy, have too much draw weight, or not enough draw length merely create a set of problems that can't be solved easily and can set an archer's progress back by weeks or months. To illustrate this I will address switching to a new bow of the same type as well as from recurve to compound and compound to recurve.

How Do I Know My Athlete Is Ready for a New Bow?

The only criterion for a new bow of the same kind is

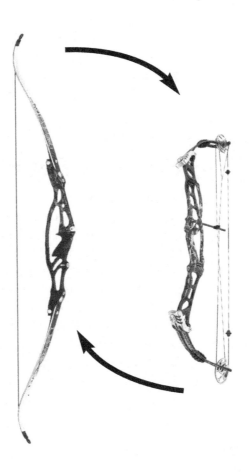

whether their current bow's performance is limiting that of the archer, the primary example being a youth who has outgrown his bow. There is a great deal of marketing hype about how "this year's bow" is better than "last year's bow," complete with claims about how much better you will shoot with the latest model. Reality tells us otherwise. The same archers tend to win year after year, typically making the transition from bow to bow as their bow sponsors crank out new models. It is in neither the manufacturer's nor the sponsored archer's interests to challenge that marketing logic and investigate whether archers would do just as well with last year's bows.

Most coaches at the elite level publically or privately admit that it is the archer, not the bow, which is responsible for the score. As long as a bow is sufficiently designed and well-made, the archer will perform about the same.

Developing archers face a different situation. Often they are using equipment that is not of the highest standard. There are a number of good reasons for this: high-end equipment is expensive, high-end equipment can be finicky to deal with (in archery vernacular it is "critical"), and young archers can grow out of equipment relatively quickly (which is why delaying the purchase of high-end arrows until they've reached full growth is also recommended).

But if the archer's equipment *is* limiting his development, it is time for an upgrade. And that is a problem. There is no way to tell ahead of time if a particular bow upgrade will equate to a performance upgrade, so some experimentation is needed. Ideally an upgrade bow can be borrowed for a few weeks to see how it goes. Often there is a healthy market for used bows which can be purchased for much less than a new one. To some extent, the quality of bows is related to price. Bows that were the top-of-the-line five or six years ago are as good now as they were then. They can be had for reasonable prices and generally have top-end fit, finish, and design. Of course, used bows may need a lot of modification and/or replacent parts to make them serviceable, so exercise caution.

Your archers will need help with these purchases and your guidance is necessary.

Fine Points When you see your archer's form and execution improving but that is not reflected in their practice or competition scores, it is time to look to the equipment. Arrows are the first thing to look at, bows are second.

How to Get Started
(Adapting to a New Bow of the Same Type)
Basic Aspects If the bow is just a different model of the same type (recurve to recurve), then it is simply a matter of transferring all of the bow accessories to the new bow (unless the old bow is being kept as a backup bow) and then the new bow must be set up, shot in, and then tuned.

Practice rounds should then be shot to see if scores improve. If they do, the archer's confidence should also increase and the equipment change was the right move. If they don't, and assuming the new bow hasn't affected form or execution, some tinkering may still be needed –

or it wasn't the equipment that was holding your archer back.

Training (Adapting to a New Bow)
No training *per se* is needed but you should allow some time to get used to the slight differences between the bows. Some healthy skepticism is warranted. Everyone likes new gear, but the proof of the pudding is in how it shoots. Encourage your archer to *prove* that the new gear is allowing higher performances.

Potential Pitfalls (Adapting to a New Bow)
1. *Disappointments May Impede Training*
Most often equipment upgrades improve performance but sometimes they do not. If the reults are disappointing, archer's can become discouraged. This may be the result of unrealistic expectations, so be sure to explain to your student how much improvement might be expected before the gear shows up.

How to Get Started
(Adapting to a New Bow of a Different Type)
Compound to Recurve
Basic Aspects This can come as a shock to some compound archers, but recurve archers experience peak draw weight at full draw, hence shooting a recurve bow is more challenging athletically than shooting a compound bow. This should be clarified long before bows are being considered for purchase. Any compound archer wishing to explore the world of recurve archery (most of the U.S. Olympians of recent history started as compound archers

or shot as one a great deal before making the switch to Olympic Recurve) should borrow a bow and receive some basic instruction on shooting it correctly beforehand.

Recurve Bows Reach Peak Draw Weight at Full Draw This has considerable consequences on archery form. Basically one cannot stay at full draw for long, so aiming is less intense, but that is to be expected as no telescopic sights, sight level bubbles, or peep sights are allowed. Archers must also adopt the archer's triangle in their upper body to create the bracing needed to be still at full draw. A compound archer's shoulders are parallel to the arrow where a recurve archer's shoulders point at her bow hand (*see illustrations*).

Recurve Bows are Lighter Having less mass, recurve bows are more easily moved around, so many archers use V-bars to stabilize their bows. Also, a full followthrough is typical as there is less bow to hold up at arm's length (*see photos*).

Clickers May Be Used in Some Styles Clickers have a poor reputation, undeservedly so. They can refine an already consistent draw length and relieve much of the decision making surrounding when to release an arrow. See "How to . . . Introduce Clickers."

Recurve to Compound

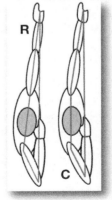

Basic Aspects The letoff built into compound bows almost feels like cheating. A recurve archer spends most of a shot at full draw weight, whereas with a compound bow, full draw weight passes in an instant between brace (zero draw weight) and holding weight (typically only 20-35% of peak weight). Extreme performance compound bows can spend most of the draw stroke at or near peak weight but such bows do not find favor with target archers who must take a great many shots in a single day (they are too tiring for the limited advantages they may offer). Compound bows are also generally possess a great deal more mass than a recurve bow, even a full kit Olympic Recurve bow, and hence stress bow shoulder muscles more.

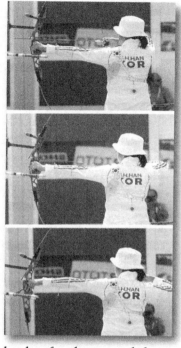

Again, a borrowed bow to develop familiarity and desirability is highly recommended before purchasing such a bow.

Compound Bows Have Letoff Because of the lower draw weight at full draw, aiming can take longer, which is a good thing since there is plenty to do if using the permitted telescopic sights, sight level bubbles, and peep sights. Also because of the letoff, the bow has it's own draw length that must be set to exactly match that of the archer. This is just one of many factors that explain why compounds involve more tinkering to get the equipment just right.

Compound Bows are Heavy The large mass is a factor in stabilizing the bow (due to inertia) so many elite compound archers cut off the feedback from their followthroughs to save having to support such a heavy object at arm's length for so long. This mass also means fewer stabilizers are needed (some use a single side rod but that is only to balance the weight of a heavier bow sight on the other side of the bow). Since more energy is loaded into the bow, more comes out of the bow as arrow speed, *and* more stays in the bow as vibration, requiring additional vibration dampening (furthur adding to the mass).

Telescopic Sighting Systems and Peep Sights Are Allowed While these are not required, the only compound form recognized in all age categories by USA Archery and World Archery allows them and they are extremely popular in the other organizations. Such systems require training and involve their own techniques and timing.

Release Aids Are Allowed in Some Styles If shooting with full kit release aids are allowed, which require their own training period and mentality adjustment.

Bonus Thrills You almost never have to string or unstring a compound bow or even check your brace height (although it is not a bad idea).

Training
(Adapting to a New Bow of a Different Type)
Some amount of training *per se* is needed mostly allowing some time to get used to the differences between the bows, especially in the timing of shots. Some healthy skepticism

is warranted. Everyone likes new gear, but the proof of the pudding is in how it shoots. Encourage your archer to *prove* that the new gear is allowing higher performances.

Potential Pitfalls
(Adapting to a New Bow of a Different Type)

1.   *Unreasonable Expectations May Create Disappointment* Just because an archer has achieved some skill with one kind of bow, doesn't mean he will achieve the same level of competence with another. Coaches need to help archers create reasonable expectations, based on their actual experience, willingness to work, and comparisons of score (practice and competition) with other archers. Expectations based on hopes are unlikely to be of much use.

Steve Ruis

19
How To . . .
Teach Relaxation

General Background Information

Archers, especially young archers, often acquire new bows. Too often these changes are unplanned in that a bow became available at a good price and they took advantage of it, or a whim was followed to "try bare-bow" or "try compound."

The physical attributes required for archery are few and, consequently, archery does not select for a particular body type. You do not have to be tall or short, light or heavy, strong or weak, quick or sluggish, or fast or slow. What you have to be able to do is: *relax and focus under the tension of a drawn bow*. While some beginning archers are quite distractible, most can muster a reasonable level of focus. As coaches we need to direct that focus on to what they are doing at any particular point in their shot and this takes a little practice and the learning of the shot sequence and the lists of what things need to be focused upon while a shot is being prepared and taken. Relaxation is a whole 'nother matter, though. Even advanced archers battle bouts of tension that infect their shots.

The reality is that relaxed shooting is repeatable shooting. Muscles that are 23.8% tense on one shot will be some different degree of tension on the next. We can't "find" 23.8% tense, but we can find "relaxed;" relaxation is the core of repeatablity.

It is important to make the point to your archers that the muscles needing to be relaxed are those not needed to make the shot. (If all their muscles were simultaneously relaxed, they would collapse in a heap.) Archers need to be standing comfortably and using only those muscles that are needed to stand stably, hold, raise, draw the bow, and finish the shot.

How Do I Know My Athlete Is Ready for a Relaxation Training?

If they are holding a bow, they are ready! Some little boys are so excited and so tense that when they try to shoot their first arrow, they can't even draw the bow. (When opposing groups of muscles, e.g. biceps and triceps, are both tensed, the joint they manipulate is locked. Posing bodybuilders are quite stiff while posing and can be pushed over easily.) Only after convincing them to relax that they can then get an arrow off. There is no such thing as "too soon" when it comes to learning to relax unused muscles while shooting.

Fine Points Obviously one begins at the beginning. Advanced relaxation exercises are inappropriate for beginners.

How to Get Started (Relaxing)

Basic Approach It is important that your archer know that being relaxed is required and then be given a mechanism for achieving this state.

With your archer on the shooting line (to associate shooting with relaxing), either holding their bow or you holding it for them, have them take their stance and then take a few deep breaths, letting each out a little slower than the inhalation. As each exhalation occurs, suggest that they should feel as if they were sinking into the ground. (They are not, but many people elevate their centers of gravity out of habit. As they relax, their center of gravity drops, and it feels like they are sinking.)

Then have them execute a good shot from this state.

The key to being relaxed when shooting is starting in a relaxed state and then maintaining the feeling. As coach, you need to look to see if tension creeps into the shot as it progresses (bow shoulders creep up, string fingers tense up, bow hands tense up). On fingers, look for white knuckles as a sure sign of tension.

Getting both hands into a relaxed state is a major stepping stone to repeatable accuracy.

Training (Relaxing)

Initial Stages You can draw attention to unwanted tension by touching those areas tensing up. (It is important that you tell your athlete you will be doing this for obvious safety reasons!) For example, fingers on the bowhand should be curled and relaxed. Outstretched fingers make for a tense palm, too, so reach out and touch those fingers and ask that they be relaxed.

Shooting blind bale (blank bale, eyes closed) can facilitate learning as it allows the student-archer to focus on his tactile senses instead of visual senses.

Another example of this is that the string/release hand should feel like it were stretching as the draw progresses.

A Potential Pitfall Some archers, when told about the "stretching string hand" illusion take something that happens and try to make it something they do. What they do is slowly let the string/release slip on their fingers. This provides a similar sensation. Be sure to check that they keep a deep hook on the string/release aid while doing this.

Later Stages There are exercises that can be used to lower tension levels. One easy one is for your student to go through their body, from the ground up, tensing muscles and then relaxing them:

Training Script
(*Slowly*) Close your eyes and tense your toes in your shoes and relax them; tense the calves of your legs and then relax them, tense your thighs and relax them, tense your stomach area/abs, etc.

Another exercise is to "shake" out the tension.

Training Script

(*Slowly*) Pick one foot up off of the ground and shake it until the leg feels loose. Repeat with the other leg. Repeat with the arms (empty-handed).

A relaxation exercise for the shoulders is: lift the shoulders up as high as possible (a big "shrug") and then lower them as far as possible, repeat two more times. (In order to get the shoulders down, the associated muscles must be relaxed, one cannot force them down.)

Many relaxation exercises are available online, a simple search will reveal them.

Potential Pitfalls (Relaxing)

1. *Allowing the string/release to slip from the fingers in order for them to feel relaxed* (see above)
2. *Tension is Hard to Recognize (Teach them to Fight Back with Relaxation)*

Body awareness is something hard to find in most archers, at least those who didn't study dance. Consequently most archers are unaware of the tension in their bodies and, especially under tournament pressure, can develop some quite bad habits of tensing the wrong muscles. A classic example is a young Olympic Recurve archer competing for the first time with a clicker. At some point, he struggles with getting through the clicker, which evokes all kinds of failure thoughts which makes him tense, which makes it harder to get through the click-er, which makes him more tense, etc. This can burn this tension into a habitual behavior hard to break. Coaches need to monitor such situations closely.

It may also be worthwhile to show your students the power of relaxation in practice by moving their clicker in a quarter of an inch and then telling them that "it will be much harder to get through their clicker now." They will almost automatically "try harder," that is tense up, and they won't be able to get through the clicker at all (certainly not with good form). Then tell them the "secret" to accomplishing this task is to relax fully and then they will be able to do it. Either have them do a few relaxation drills or just encourage them to relax through the shot and they should be able to get through it (the basis of this lesson is that the clicker should be set so that the archer can pull their arrow point, with good form, one quarter of an inch past the clicker). Tell him that the "secret" solution when they begin to fight their clicker is "to relax."

How To's . . .

New
Experiences

Field Archery is a little like golf in that there is a sequence of targets set at different distances that one proceeds to shoot. This is an NFAA shoot with the targets scored 5-4-3, four arrows per target. In this instance, there is one target for each of the four members of this group of competitors.

20
How To . . .
Introduce Field Archery

General Background Information

Most beginners learn target archery on a target field, but if there is a field range nearby, participating in field archery is a viable, fun, and instructive activity. Because field ranges are hard to set up, only permanent ranges are available today. (Ranges have been set up for a single event and then taken down in the past.)

Field archery is based on simulated hunting scenarios and is like golf in that there are a number of targets shot in serial order at different distances and different-sized target faces. The most common field ranges in the U.S. are set up according to National Field Archery Association (NFAA) rules but 3-D ranges are increasing in popularity. The NFAA courses have targets at distances ranging from 7-80 yards to with several sizes and styles of targets. Archers move in groups from one target to the next. Most commonly four arrows are shot at each target and scored. A short walk (usually just a few steps) takes the group to the shooting stake of the next target. Field archery games are typically in multiples of 14 targets.

How Do I Know My Athlete Is Ready for Field Archery?

Field archery is fun and all an archer needs to be able to do is shoot with basic form to enjoy it. You can take a group around a field course with them only carrying their bows and armguards and you carrying all of their arrows. Participation in a

Kids love field archery!

tournament, though, requires the ability to shoot the quantity of arrows needed to finish.

How to Get Started (Field Archery)

Basic Steps If a field trip is not yet feasible, a small field course can be setup on a target range that you control. This can be used to teach the rules of field archery as well as providing experience shooting at widely spaced targets. This may be precluded by range safety considerations, so all of the targets set up may have to be parallel to one another, and shot in the normal direction for your field. Even so, different sized targets can be shot at different distances in a rough simulation of field archery.

Training (Field Archery)

Initial Stages Field targets (paper) can be introduced into practice and shot at, providing discussions as to aiming and scoring (NFAA "Hunter" (*right*) targets have few points of aim available on the target faces, for example).

Later Stages After some basic orientation, or a few targets being shot on a simulated range, a field trip is the best way to experience field archery for the first time. Even inviting a student to a field competition can be used as a first experience.

If you opt for a field trip, contact your field archery club about the use of their range. You may have to pay guest fees to shoot. Oftentimes a member will volunteer to take you around and show your students his range. Most members are proud of all of the hard work they put into building and maintaining their range.

Realize that you may be quite far from help if there is a problem. A first aid kit is a must, along with some basic tools to make any field repairs needed.

Potential Pitfalls (Field Archery)

1. *You May Be Far from Help When Problems Arise*
If a medical emergency occurs while you are on the field, you may be quite far from help. Be sure to carry a map of the range or get an orientation ahead of time. Consult with a club member about cell phone service, 9-1-1 service, etc. and be sure that you know how to get to the closest hospital. Since you are the coach, archers will look to you for all of this and even though the likelihood of any of these things happening is quite low, being prepared is essential. A first-aid kit is a must.

Photo by Gary Holstein

21

How To...

Introduce Target Archery

General Background Information

Some archers are first taught at a field range or a 3-D range and have never experienced a target tournament. Target archery (*see photo left*) is shot on a flat field (generally facing north to preclude problems with the sun) with all of the archers standing on the same shooting line (sometimes there are so many archers they have to shoot in shifts called "lines"). The targets are placed at various distances based on gender and age classifications but the distances shot are quite far. On an NFAA field range, adults shoot more than half of their shots inside 40 yards. On a target range most of the shots are well over 40 yards for adults. The FITA International Round, shot for many decades in Olympic competition, was 144 arrows with adult men shooting 36 arrows at each of four targets at 90, 70, 50, and 30 meters.

Target archery generally has high arrow counts at longer distances.

How Do I Know My Athlete Is Ready for Target Archery?

Target archery is fun and all an archer needs to be able to do is shoot with basic form to enjoy it. Participation in a tournament, though, requires the ability to shoot the quantity of arrows needed to finish.

How to Get Started (Target Archery)

Basic Steps If a trip to a target range is not yet feasible, a small target course can be setup on a field range that you control. This can be used to teach the rules of target archery as well as getting your student(s) experience shooting at different targets at longer distances. This may be precluded by range safety considerations. Even so, different targets can be shot at different distances in a rough simulation of target archery.

Training (Target Archery)

Initial Stages Target archery targets (paper) can be introduced into practice and shot at, providing discussions as to aiming and scoring. Some organizations require all arrow holes to be marked prior to pulling. Practicing these things can lend comforting familiarity to a somewhat strange new experience, especially if preparing for a tournament.

See the pretty colors? Target archery targets are multi-colored (white, black, blue, red, gold from outside in) with each color comprising two scoring rings.

Later Stages After some basic orientation, even a few targets being shot on a simulated range, a field trip is the best way to experience target archery for the first time. Since there are very few permanent target ranges in the U.S., inviting a student to a target competition can be used as a first experience. They could go as a competitor or a spectator.

The joy of target archery is you stay put in the same locale all day. So, you can bring folding chairs to sit on, a cooler for drinks and snacks, toolboxes for any repairs needed, etc. People often bring pop-up tent shades because there can be limited shade in many venues and the high arrow counts, mean you can be there most of the day.

Potential Pitfalls (Target Archery)

1. *You May Be Far from Help When Problems Arise*
If a medical emergency occurs while you are on the field, you may be quite far from help. Consult with a club member about cell phone service, 9-1-1 service, etc. and be sure that you know how to get to the closest hospital. Since you are the coach, archers will look to you for all of this and even though the likelihood of any of these things happening is quite low, being prepared is essential. A first-aid kit is a must.

Photo by Andy Macdonald

22
How To . . .
Introduce Competition

General Background Information

Competition at archery tournaments is the cauldron of excellence. Flaws in archer's technique are exposed and lessons abound therefrom. Competing in several different types of archery (target, field, 3-D) expands an archer's understanding of her own technique and can lead to changing goals. Many compound archers, having experienced target archery for the first time, realize that they may be interested in international competition representing their country.

The most common scenario in which a recreational archer (who only shoots for fun) discovers that they are really a competitive archer (who wants to learn to win) is by going to a tournament, doing well, and thinking "if I worked at this I could be really good."

And for most archers, competition is fun (but not for all; for some it is agony).

How Do I Know My Athlete Is Ready for a Competition?

Once an archer has enough kit (bow and enough arrows, quiver, etc.) the easiest test of readiness is to invite your athlete to attend one. If they are unsure, ask them to go and observe. (Some are easier to observe than others: indoor and target events are on the easy end, 3-D and field are on the harder end.)

First tournaments should best involve low arrow counts and a relaxed venue, so local events are best. Some archers experience their first competitions at state championship shoots but it is hard to come up with reasons why that would be preferred.

How to Get Started
(Participating in a Competition)

Basic Preparation The more you can prepare your athletes for a tournament, the better their chances of having a good experience. Showing pictures from last year's event is helpful. Providing a checklist of everything they need to bring and do is very useful. Explaining the rules is important, but simplify them for your archers. For example, if a timing system is used explain the system but simplify it for them by suggesting that they don't do anything until someone else has, e.g. don't go to the shooting line until someone else has, don't shoot until someone else has, etc. Also, tell them that it is okay to ask questions, but limit these to between ends. Any archer who is willing to tell others that "this is my first tournament," will find many people helping them when it is needed.

Training (Participating in a Competition)

Initial Stages Make sure your students know basic rules (no touching of arrows or target until scoring is done, how to score, how to call in a Judge, etc.). These can be taught during practice especially in the form of little contests if you are working with more than one archer at a time.

Later Stages After your archers are familiar with the basics, small mock tournaments (*e.g.* three ends) can be staged, even full-scale (all of the bells and whistles) mock tournaments if you have the wherewithal to do that.

Hesitant students can go on a field trip to visit a tournament, but if you go as coach to explain things you should be compensated.

Preparation is the key, but avoid overwhelming athletes with too many "do's and don'ts."

We recommend that athletes have two goals for their first tournament (actually for all tournaments): one is a deportment goal, the other an outcome goal. One possible deportment goal is "I will ask questions when they occur to me." The best possible outcome goal for a first tournament is "I will have fun." Later, these goals are drafted between coach and athlete based on the archer's experience at such competitions.

Potential Pitfalls (Participating in a Competition)

1. *Tournament "Pressure" Can Cause and Burn In Bad Habits*

Before an archer's form matures and becomes stable, tournament pressure can create bad habits. The intensity of the situation can burn in these bad habits and require a great deal of work to unlearn. Tournament pressure is entirely self-created and some archers throw themselves into that cauldron head first. We have seen first tournament archers lose focus, talk trash(!), and even freeze almost to the point of immobility. Coaches need to be aware that a wide range of problems may crop up and learn to deal with them.

The key thing is for their athletes to relax and focus on their shots. They need to realize that nothing can be done about a shot arrow, only about their next one. They need to learn that nothing good comes from obsessing about their score. All of their scores at their first tournament will be personal bests.

Who Competes? Against Whom or What?

We make a distinction between *recreational* archers and *competitive* archers. While both types of archers appear at an archery competition and be shooting side-by-side, the difference between the two is the competitive archer is training with the goal of winning the competition while the recreation archer's are simply to participate, to enjoy the shooting, to test him- or herself, and almost always to "have fun," and so forth.

Competitive archers undergo rigorous physical training, equipment testing, and high arrow count shooting sessions as regular aspects of their practice. Recreational archers are unlikely to do such things.

Still, recreational archers should be encouraged to attend competitions because they are fun and instructive and one never knows when a recreational archer might just decide he or she would like to learn how to win. Competitions are instructive, for example, in that the pressure can illuminate flaws in their technique. This benefits both kinds of archers.

There are many ways to compete, that don't involve a goal of "winning." Here are a few examples.

Competing Against Oneself Archery is a sport in which there is no defense. In this it is like golf and trapshooting. Consequently, the only person you can triumph over is . . . yourself. This is done by keeping track of one's personal best score, often called just a "personal best" or PB for short. If your PB goes up on a particular round on a consistent basis, you are making considerable improvement in your archery whether that score is close to a winning score or not.

Competing Against Record Scores You can set scoring goals as a percent of a record score, *e.g.* 75% or 90% of a particular round's local, state, or national record. (Your archer gets to choose which based on how ambitious they are.) Knowing that they can shoot a high percentage of a record score is a solid indicator of achievement, as well as an indicator that they are capable. The record scores themselves include handicapping for the ages, types of equipment, and genders of the archers involved, which makes these comparisons valid. Traditional archers can even compete against famous archers of the past as records have been kept for hundreds of years.

Competing Against Fellow Competitors Archery is a social sport and part of that is friendly competitions. An archer picks someone about equal in ability (or not!) and poses a competition. This can be during practice or at a formal competitive event. If the two archers are of different skill levels, a "handicap" (typically as a number of points) is negotiated. A prize for winning the contest is also negotiated, most commonly the loser buys the winner a can of soda. (Competing for things worth more than this is discouraged.)

Competing Against the Field Attending a competition sponsored by an archery organization to test oneself against the field can result in a recreational archer becoming a competitive archer. This has happened time and time again. An archer shows up and competes and shocks herself by placing very high. The idea that enhanced training might put the archer on top of the field can lead to higher level competitions, more intense practices, specialized coaching, physical and mental training, etc.—and the transformation into a competitive archer has begun.

You can help your archers learn by encouraging them to attend competitions and also asking them to write down what they learn from these. Suggest that your archers make two lists for each competition (to be written within 24 hours of the end of the competition): *List #1:* What did I learn at this competition? and *List #2:* What will I do differently at the next competition? A minimum of three answers to each of these questions needs to be written in a notebook. One reinforces current learning and the other guides practice going forward.

Appendices

Steve Ruis

Having a Written Coaching Philosophy

Every coach should write down their coaching philosophy because, for one, you have one whether you have written it down or not and it may surprise you when you see it in writing, and two, prospective customers/archers may want to see it. Here's an example:

My Coaching Philosophy
Steve Ruis
Last Updated Summer 2013

Because archery is not just an individual sport but is also a sport with no opponent, almost all of the responsibility for a performance falls to the athlete. Consequently my goal is to create a situation in which the athlete becomes functionally self-sufficient. To do this, I:

- Describe my general approach (bring all parts of an archer's shot up to parity and then rework the shot as many times as is desired to achieve the archer's goals) but am open to other approaches an archer may desire.
- Endeavor to explain everything I am asking an athlete to do (but only up to the point they desire).

- Ask the athlete to make all final decisions regarding form changes, etc.
- Continually educate athletes in techniques that can be used to self-educate himself, *e.g.* process goals, journaling, learning how to analyze video (but only up to the point they desire).
- Break down complex tasks into doable parts as much as possible, explaining to the athlete what is being done and why.
- Demonstrate a positive outlook, which is a requirement of successful coaching as much as successful archery.
- Educate the archer on his/her equipment with the goal of them taking full responsibility for their own equipment.
- Educate the archer on the requirements of competing successfully with the goal of them taking full responsibility for competition planning, preparation, and execution.
- Honor the athlete's outcome goals and teach how ladders of success and careful preparation and execution are used to achieve them.
- Honor the fact that each student is a unique individual and that I may or may not be a major or even minor influence on their lives.
- Work as hard for my students as they do for themselves. If a student does not want to work toward their own goals, I will honor their decision but I will not continue to work with them.
- Will endeavor to point out how what they are learning from their bow and arrows carries over into other

aspects of their lives.

- Will work with parents of underage athletes, necessarily, so that there is full communication between and among the archer's support team.
- Work hard to improve my knowledge, skills, and attitudes as a coach.

This is updated from time to time. S. P. Ruis

Steve Ruis

Coaching Rationales

All coaches should be able to explain why they do what they do and the ways that they do it. Here are some of mine.

1. *Introduction of archery with stretch band/form strap* Some coaches insist the only way to introduce archery is with mimetics (play acting like air guitar), and using aids such as stretch bands and nonstreching straps. Their argument is that until a beginning archer-athlete understands what to do their bow, the arrow, and the target simply interfere with learning the appropriate body positions and movements.

    Rationale I don't disagree with the approach, but I disagree that this is the only way to introduce archery. These coaches are confusing the training of a serious competitive archer with someone looking for recreation. Our argument is summed up with a couple of questions: "How can we know if someone is a serious competitive archer unless we let them try it?" and "If they don't have fun right away, how long do you think they would continue?" We are in the business of helping people become recreational archers and then offering them competitive archery if they are interested. I am unaware of a "stretch band/form strap" approach that doesn't involve a captive audience (typically in school), an audience which does not have the option to quit, or consists of archers who have made the commitment to become a competitive archer.

And, if you agree with this approach, and the archers allow, it can be used.

2. *Introduction of bow and arrow one-on-one and up close to a target*

Why are new archers started up so close to such a big target?

Rationale Most children are introduced to archery by shooting arrows at a "fun shoot" or camp activity. Once children have shot arrows it is more difficult to start their formal instruction with a stretch band or form strap. This does not mean you cannot try. Shooting arrows is fun, especially when they hit the target. We start beginners up close at a fairly large target. The idea is for the archers to experience success, here in the form of the arrows hitting the target. This is not a "lowering of the bar" but, at least in part, training of the archer's self image to expect that the archer's arrows will hit the target and always at, or near, the center. As the archer progresses in developing consistent form, targets are moved farther away or replaced with smaller target faces at the same distance until the archer is at standard-sized targets, at standard shooting distances.

The goals at this stage are simple: not hitting the bow arm with the bow string and learning basic archery safety (arrows always point to the target, bows are only drawn on the shooting line (or under the direction of a coach), how to pull arrows, etc.) These goals can be accomplished in this format while beginners are having fun . . . shooting arrows.

3. ***Introduction of a finger tab***
Why is the finger tab introduced so late?

Rationale A finger tab assists in ensuring correct finger placement on the bow string, preventing finger soreness, and in providing a slick surface for the string to slide off. Typical program (= inexpensive) finger tabs are counterproductive in that they do not fit and are too stiff and, therefore, make a beginning archer more clumsy. The very low starting draw weight generally allows archers to shoot fairly well without a finger tab. As the draw weight goes up, so does the tension in the bowstring, and consequently the pressure on the fingers, so soreness can develop. A quality finger tab costs only about $10 and can be fitted to the archer by acquiring the correct size then trimming excess material away. The clumsy stage is avoided until the student knows they are interested enough in archery to buy their own tab.

4. ***Aiming***
Why are you teaching point of aim aiming techniques? Why not just start them on a sight right away?

Rationale Grouping while shooting "instinctively" is required first, before any aiming technique is taught. Teaching aiming techniques of any kind without grouping is pointless as the focus on aiming detracts from the focus on shooting correctly. The point of aim (POA) methods supply archers with consistent feedback on their shots. For example, with POA instruction, if an archer's groups are left or right of center, the feedback addresses body alignment, stance, and especially anchor position. If the archer's groups are above or below the center, the feedback indicates an incorrect point of aim. If the archer's groups are spread out vertically, an inconsistent draw length is indicated. All of this feedback informs archers as to the flaws in their shots.

The reasons for teaching POA are: a) students want to aim, b) bow sights need to be set up (with no little effort) for each student (which means the best time to do this is when they get their own equipment), c) it is easier to introduce sights after a student has an idea of what a sight picture is, has learned to focus on his body as well as the sight, and has learned good head position and alignment, and d) some archers don't ever use sights.

5. *Introduction of a simple stabilizer*
   Why is the long stabilizer the one emphasized?
   Rationale The focus is on the long rod (used in Olympic-Recurve and Compound Unlimited (NFAA: FS) and Compound Limited (NFAA: FSL) as well as NFAA Barebow) for practical reasons (shorter stabilizers do not have much of an effect without adding a great deal of weight to the bow). Students who wish to shoot a style that uses a short stabilizer certainly may.

6. ### *Introduction of a sling*
    Why not put a sling on the archers right away?

    Rationale The bow sling has two purposes: a preventative for "grabbing the bow" and to encourage a relaxed bow hand. Based on coach's preference, slings can be introduced before stabilizers.

    There are three common styles of sling (finger, wrist, bow). Korean coaches recommend finger slings, Coach Vittorio Frangilli recommends wrist slings, and compound archers prefer bow slings. Which one any archer prefers is up to them. Slings are introduced later, rather than earlier as they make archers clumsier and require advanced technique ("Let the sling catch the bow.") which is better learned after a stabilizer (if any) is introduced because stabilizers change bow reaction, i.e. followthrough bow behavior substantially.

7. ### *Introduction of a bow sight*
    Why are sights (for those who want them) introduced so late?

    Rationale Until a beginning archer has fairly steady form, the focus on aiming that is inherent in the use of a bow sight can detract from learning good form. Having learned to aim off of the point allows a progressive entry into the use of a bow sight. For example, students who have a good point of aim at a close-in target can learn to use a sight by shooting POA (ignoring the bow sight's aperture/pin), then after several shots noticing the position of the sight aperture. The aperture is moved until when sighting

POA correctly, the aperture is centered on the target in the archer's field of vision. The two sight pictures now represent the same "aim" and either should result in arrows landing in the center of the target. Students achieving proficiency (smaller groups) are then moved back incrementally without moving the aperture and the change in the point of impact is noted. In this manner students learn the relationships between aperture positions, impact points, and distances.

In other words, students have already learned how to aim, now they are learning how "to sight." It is much easier to do this in stages that all at once.

8. *Introduction of a release aid*
   My kid wants to shoot a release but you have got him shooting "fingers," how come?

   Rationale Release aids are complicated in and of themselves. If we add that complication to archery form that is shaky, everything will be affected. If bad habits are created, they will be hard to break. So, we get an archer into full kit, except the release aid, shooting well off of the string, then we introduce release aids. Also, releases are expensive and must be fitted and adjusted, only then training can occur, beginning with a rope loop or form strap with loop of release rope added. It is probably a very good idea to start everyone on a triggerless release aid as this removes the step of triggering the release from the learning task. Then, after a reasonable release technique is learned, a trigger release can be introduced with only the operation of the trigger to be learned.

9. *Introduction of a clicker*

Everybody else recommends you put a clicker on an Olympic-style bow early, why don't you?

Rationale Clickers provide draw length control and shot timing control. If properly used, the decision to release the arrow occurs subconsciously rather than consciously. I don't know what "everybody else recommends" but the Korean method has young archers shooting thousands upon thousands of arrows before the clicker is introduced. The idea is to make sure an archer's form is stable before introducing something new. Nothing disrupts learning more than having many confusing things to deal with at the same time.

We also believe that the clicker has a reputation of being "hard" or "hard to learn." We believe this is because no one else seems to use a systematic approach in teaching it. We do.

10. *Compound Rests*

My kid still has a cheap, plastic rest on his bow, why don't you recommend a launcher rest?

Rationale We do recommend a launcher rest . . . when it will have some effect. The plastic screw-in arrow rest we advocate is fine for quite a while . . . and is indeed inexpensive. If you want to buy your child a birthday present and are willing to install and set up the rest, we certainly have no objection, but don't expect a big performance boost from it. Our philosophy is that learning to shoot well is far more effective than trying to find bow accessories that will make you shoot better (because there are none). There is a point, though, where an increase in the quality of an accessory allows for better technique or simply better performance. We try to balance the two when introducing equipment modifications.

11. *Introduction of peep sight*

My daughter already has a sight but she doesn't have a peep sight to go with it? Why not?

Rationale A peep sight completes the "aiming package" for compound bow archers who choose to use a bow sight by creating a rear site for both windage and elevation. It is taught later because if included at the same time as the bow sight is introduced there would be too many points of focus to be addressed simultaneously, resulting in unnecessary confusion. In effect, a new step is being added to the student's shot sequence and the order and execution of the step need to be emphasized before an outcome becomes the focus of the archer's attention.

12. *Introduction of a cushion plunger*

I think my daughter needs a cushion plunger; can I buy her one?

Rationale A cushion plunger may be introduced any time after the bow and arrows are acquired as it can be set up by the coach simply to provide some side pressure to arrows and to set centershot. Since there is no reason to expect a noticeable improvement based on installing a cushion plunger until an archer's form is quite solid, we feel it can be introduced quite later. Tuning with the plunger should be left to when fine bow tuning is addressed. Another reason is a cheap plunger and mechanical arrow rest might cost $30-$40, with expensive ones being $100-$150. The screw-in plastic rest works fine and only costs about $3, so we suggest you wait. (In this manner athletes "earn" their equipment upgrades by learning and dedication, both good lessons.)

Steve Ruis

Mental Program Rationales

Introducing the metal aspects of archery differs slightly from introducing the physical aspects of shooting arrows in that the physical and equipment learning tasks that are apparent in the physical shooting of arrows do not line up exactly with an archer's mental environment. Consequently, introducing mental skills is more closely involved with an evaluation of the archer's mental capabilities as discerned by the coach than anything necessarily physical in nature. So, after the introduction of a shot sequence (which provides a framework for mental instruction), other skills can be introduced based on archer aptitude and preference. In other words, which skills will be learned and in what sequence depend upon the student's readiness.

1. *Introduction of the shot sequence*
   Why do beginners have to do this shot sequence thing with a stretch band?

   Rationale An archer's mental instruction must start with the introduction and use of a shot sequence/routine as each step of the sequence has physical sensations and thoughts that go along with them. The sum total of those thoughts is an archer's mental program. A shot sequence provides a framework and set of terms that allows archer and coach to discuss various phases of a shot. Note that *when* you have thoughts during a shot is as important as *what* those thoughts are. Whenever anything physical or mental goes wrong (like thinking about one's stance while at full draw or something from outside intruding on the shot) a let down is required. This is the beginning of a disciplined mental system. Without such discipline, no other mental skills will be of much use.

Note to Coaches Do not get drawn into a debate of how many steps there are in a shot sequence; the only correct number is "more than one." There are some who insist there are only a few steps in a shot sequence but these folks always have short lists of things to do within each step, which are in reality additional steps buried in the "short" list. The number of steps can be changed as needed to place more or less focus on a particular step or steps. So, one archer's sequence will differ from another's and an individual archer's sequence may differ from one year to the next.

Key Points Learning the basic sequence with a stetch band rather than with the stress of the draw weight of the bow allows archers time to think when practicing it. The steps must be performed separately before blending is allowed (such as blending the raising of the bow with the draw, for instance). This is necessary to make sure all physical checkpoints and shot thoughts are properly attached to the sequence in their correct order in time. Later, this is of value when something goes wrong with an archer's shot: the archer can revert to their "fundamentals," the step-by-step shot sequence, to diagnose and solve the problem.

2. *Introduction of self-talk*
My kid says you want them to talk to themselves. What's up with that?
   Rationale We don't ask student-archers to talk to themselves, but if they do, we ask them to talk nicely. Positive self-talk is easy to teach, effective, and is a skill that can be translated to behavior with others (treat yourself respectfully, treat others respectfully). In essence, we are teaching them how to teach themselves.

3. *Introduction of process/deportment goals*
These kids just want to have fun, why do they have to have goals?
   Rationale Goals are introduced only when students equate "having fun" with "getting better," that is they have stated the goal of becoming a better archer. Goal setting is an important skill . . . for goal-oriented people. Even for student-archers who aren't particularly focused by goals can be affected by the process. The easiest way is by associating the process with participation in competitions.
   Students can opt out of the program and just shoot for fun at any time.

4. *Introduction to imagery*
Why are you messing with my kid's head with all this imagineering stuff?
   Rationale As children we played games of imagina-

tion: "bottom of the ninth, last game of the World Series, two outs, score is 5-2 and the bases are loaded, and Smith comes to bat (crowd roars)." Why did we do that? Does a ten-year old really want to be in that situation? The answer is clearly "no" (most ten-year olds would faint to be in the batter's box with 95 mph fastballs zooming by their heads). We are simply preparing to be "in the spotlight" at some point in some athletic contest and we are imagining everything going well (we either strike "Smith" out if we are the pitcher or, if we are Smith, we hit a home run). Imagination is essentially synthetic experience and it has a valid role in archery. There is a good deal of evidence that if a shot (good or bad) is imagined just before being attempted, the actual shot is more likely to resemble the imagined shot and its corresponding outcome than a shot in which no imagining occurs. Obviously most people would prefer imagining a perfect shot than an awful one.

Imagery is a life skill that has applications in many other situations. Of course, any student can modify their Individual Curriculum Plan if any part of it conflicts with their religion, personal mores, or fundamental beliefs.

5. **Introduction to affirmations**
Are these affirmation cards going to give my kid a swelled head?

Rationale We all like it when others say nice things about us. Affirmations are saying "nice" things to ourselves, a "nice" statement that conveys a message. Just as lies told often enough start to sound like truth, truths that haven't been realized yet can also sound like the truth. In essence, a story is being written that hasn't happened yet. Stories teach. A political campaign that states "Yes, We Can!" isn't saying much clearly but delivers a very powerful message.

6. **Introduction to shot thoughts**
I have never heard this "shot thoughts" idea and I have been around archery for 40 years!

Rationale The concept of "shot thoughts" was borrowed from golfers who use "swing thoughts" to help keep their golf swings and putting strokes consistent. Shot thoughts are short, powerful strings of words ("strong boow arm") attached to particular parts of the shot sequence to make those steps more consistent or to correct those steps for a flaw that has crept into them. Archers have been using this technique for decades.

7. **Introduction to shot timing**
My wife has me timing her with a stop watch while she shoots. Nobody at my archery club is doing that, why is she?

Rationale Everyone shoots in a particular cadence or rhythm. Archer's who shoot higher scores "in rhythm" are considered "rhythm shooters," but everyone benefits (and "rhythm shooters" even more) in making their shot rhythm regular. This is a protection against the pressure of situations like shoot-offs as well as a general aid in shooting well.

The process consists of finding what one's own rhythm is and then finding a mental tool to keep it or regain it when lost. Often snatches of songs that have rhythms similar to an archer's shot rhythm can be used as part of the archer's shot sequence to help lock it in. If you don't like the stopwatch, other tools are available (such as metronomes).

Notes

_____

_____

_____

_____

_____

_____

_____

_____

_____

_____

_____

_____

_____

_____

_____

_____

_____

Notes

Notes

Notes

Notes

_____

_____

_____

_____

_____

_____

_____

_____

_____

_____

_____

_____

_____

_____

_____

_____

_____

About the Author

Steve Ruis is an avid archer and coach. He has a Level 4 Coaching Certificate from USA Archery and a Master Coach Certificate from the National Field Archery Association and recently became certified by U.S. Collegiate Archery. Since 1999, he has been the editor of *Archery Focus* magazine which is distributed worldwide and was at one point being translated into Italian, French, German, and Spanish. He has written numerous articles about archery and coaching for that magazine and for others. He has medalled in national- and state-level competitions but his proudest archery accomplishment is being a three-time club champion of the Nevada County Sportsmens Club (Nevada City, CA). He is co-author/editor of *Precision Archery* (with Claudia Stevenson) which has sold over 17,000 copies. More recently he has written *Coaching Archery, More on Coaching Archery, Even More on Coaching Archery, Archery for Kids,* and *A Parent's Guide to Archery, Winning Archery, Why You Suck at Archery, and Shooting Arrows (Archery for Adult Beginners).*

More On Coaching Archery!

Following up on his first coaching book, **Coaching Archery**, which was written to help beginning to intermediate coaches, **Steve Ruis** has a new offering to archery coaches everywhere. This time, the topics are on the full gamet of coaching topics which range from the role of emotion in the making of an archery shot, to teaching a shot sequence, to biomechanics,  and how coaches should treat their athletes (and one another) as well as five major chapters on what is missing from the archery coaching profession.

Each topic is covered in a short chapter which is easy to digest but which provides a great deal of food for thought. If you are thinking of becoming a coach or already are an archery coach and are looking for some new ideas and help with dealing with the logistics of coaching, this is the book for you.

Get your copy of **More On Coaching Archery** today!

280 pages • ISBN 978-0-9821471-8-4 • US $24.95

For All Archery Coaches!

Even More On Coaching Archery!

Following hard on the heels of **More on Coaching Archery**, which was written to help all archery coaches, **Steve Ruis** has a new offering to archery coaches everywhere. As in MOCA, the topics are on the full gamet of coaching topics including form recommendations, biomechanics, coaching students based upon their personality type, how to  "look" at students (what to look for), archery drills, watching out for words that don't instruct, and many, many more. Two chapters are even devoted to adapting standards form, that is how to make adjustments to the textbook form you are taught in coach trainings.

Each topic is covered in a short chapter which is easy to digest but which provides a great deal of food for thought. If you benefited from reading **More on Coaching Archery**, expect more of the same!

Get your copy of **Even More On Coaching Archery** today!

244 pages • ISBN 978-0-9848860-7-4 • US $24.95

For All Archery Coaches!

Printed in Great Britain
by Amazon